One of the brutally hard lessons I had to learn as a young pastor was this: For Americans aged forty and under, the spiritual disciplines are pretty much gone. And in the digital age—when multinational corporations such as Apple, Google, and Facebook are spending billions of dollars to make distraction and addiction the new normal—we desperately need to reawaken these ancient practices. After all, the way of Jesus is just that—a way of life. I'm thrilled to see Daniel, my fellow Pacific Northwest pastor, writing about these very practices. I deeply believe they are key to the future of the church.

JOHN MARK COMER
Pastor for teaching and vision at Bridgetown Church and author of *God Has a Name*

A life committed to loving God, loving self, and loving others—upward, inward, outward—is an art. Daniel Fusco is a winsome and pastoral guide on this journey, which will leave you "insanely hopeful."

ROBERT GELINAS
Lead pastor of Colorado Community Church

I always appreciate the unique way in which Daniel nuances the basic truth about life. He tackles difficult issues with grace and simplicity and helps us all look more intently at Jesus.

JEREMY CAMP
Songwriter and recording artist

Author, pastor, and musician Daniel Fusco writes like the jazz musician he is—and you ca

into the dynamic rhythm and sway of his words about life with the King of kings. Fusco takes you on an energetic and fun journey through the greatest commandment, inviting you to connect intimately with God and with others and encouraging all of us to lead lives of passion and legacy—all to the glory of our creative and wonderful Jesus.

AUBREY SAMPSON
Author of *Overcomer: Breaking Down the Walls of Shame and Rebuilding Your Soul*

Ever since I first met Daniel, I have been blessed by his commitment to Scripture, his passion for the lost, and his dedication to the church. He is a gifted teacher, an engaging communicator, and a humble follower of Jesus who wants nothing more than to see others thrive in their own walks with God. I'm excited to see how God uses this book to inspire, challenge, and motivate others to live into their fullest potential in Christ.

LUIS PALAU
World evangelist and author of *Out of the Desert . . . Into the Life God Fully Intended*

This is a grace-filled, gospel-focused, joy-inducing book that will deepen your walk with Jesus. I'm grateful for Daniel's work and inspiring passion.

DR. PHILIP NATION
Pastor and author of *Habits for Our Holiness*

In his newest book, *Upward, Inward, Outward*, Daniel Fusco takes us beyond the *theory* of loving God and others and into the practical *reality* of what it means to do so daily. I encourage you to let him guide you through three of the most important things we're called to do: love God, love ourselves, and love others. You'll be glad you did.

LARRY OSBORNE
Pastor of North Coast Church and author of *Sticky Teams*

With the same finesse, expertise, and splash of funk he famously exhibits on the bass guitar, Pastor Daniel Fusco has composed a virtual discipleship jam session in *Upward, Inward, Outward*. It's simple, rich, and foundational—not unlike the gospel it explains.

JESSIE MINASSIAN
Blogger at LifeLoveandGod.com and author of *Unashamed* and *Family*

This book is important. It's beautifully written because Daniel writes about what's important to Jesus—love. As you read this book, you will become more loving toward God, yourself, and others.

DERWIN L. GRAY
Pastor of Transformation Church and author of *Limitless Life: You Are More Than Your Past When God Holds Your Future*

Our identity drives our activity, and when we know who God is and who he says we are, it changes everything. In this book Pastor Daniel Fusco does a phenomenal job helping us learn the art of loving God, loving ourselves, and loving people through different lenses such as worship, fasting, and community.

LEVI LUSKO
Pastor of Fresh Life Church and author of *Through the Eyes of a Lion*

It's not enough to just know the right things—God wants to help us walk in what we know. Daniel Fusco shares spiritual truths in ways we can all respond to, understand, and grasp. He does it again in this new book, sharing some of the most important ways we can follow Jesus.

MATT BROWN
Evangelist, author, and founder of Think Eternity

Daniel has written a book that is dripping with truth, love, and audacity. This is a book everyone needs to read over and over again.

JARRID WILSON
Pastor and author of *Love Is Oxygen*

This book will revolutionize your thinking and help revive every area of your life. Daniel's authenticity takes us on a journey toward living the life God intended for you—upward, inward, outward—which will give you the inspiration to strengthen your relationship with Jesus regardless of where you are in your faith walk.

TIM TIMBERLAKE
Author of *Abandon* and pastor of Christian Faith Center

Upward, Inward, Outward

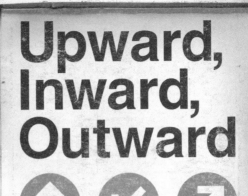

Love God
Love yourself
Love others

Daniel Fusco

with D. R. Jacobsen

Barry
You are loved!

A NavPress resource published in alliance
with Tyndale House Publishers, Inc.

NAVPRESS ⬭.

NavPress is the publishing ministry of The Navigators, an international Christian organization and leader in personal spiritual development. NavPress is committed to helping people grow spiritually and enjoy lives of meaning and hope through personal and group resources that are biblically rooted, culturally relevant, and highly practical.

For more information, visit www.NavPress.com.

Upward, Inward, Outward: Love God. Love Yourself. Love Others.

Copyright © 2017 by Daniel Fusco. All rights reserved.

A NavPress resource published in alliance with Tyndale House Publishers, Inc.

NAVPRESS and the NAVPRESS logo are registered trademarks of NavPress, The Navigators, Colorado Springs, CO. *TYNDALE* is a registered trademark of Tyndale House Publishers, Inc. Absence of ® in connection with marks of NavPress or other parties does not indicate an absence of registration of those marks.

The Team:
Don Pape, Publisher
Caitlyn Carlson, Acquisitions Editor
Helen Macdonald, Copyeditor
Julie Chen, Designer

Cover photograph of subway copyright © littleny/Adobe Stock. All rights reserved.

Author photograph taken by Crossroads Church, copyright © 2015. All rights reserved.

Published in association with the literary agency D. C. Jacobson & Associates LLC, an Author Management Company. www.dcjacobson.com.

All Scripture quotations, unless otherwise indicated, are taken from the Holy Bible, *New International Version,*® *NIV.*® Copyright © 1973, 1978, 1984, 2011 by Biblica, Inc.® Used by permission. All rights reserved worldwide.

Scripture quotations marked ESV are taken from *The Holy Bible*, English Standard Version® (ESV®), copyright © 2001 by Crossway, a publishing ministry of Good News Publishers. Used by permission. All rights reserved.

Some of the anecdotal illustrations in this book are true to life and are included with the permission of the persons involved. All other illustrations are composites of real situations, and any resemblance to people living or dead is purely coincidental.

For information about special discounts for bulk purchases, please contact Tyndale House Publishers at csresponse@tyndale.com, or call 1-800-323-9400.

Cataloging-in-Publication Data is available.

ISBN 978-1-63146-390-7

Printed in the United States of America

23	22	21	20	19	18	17
7	6	5	4	3	2	1

Thank you, Father, Son, and Spirit,

for inviting me to live and love

upward, inward, and outward.

Thank you for my beautiful family—

Lynn, Obadiah, Maranatha, and Annabelle—

who fill my world with such life!

Contents

prelude

IF YOU'RE READING THIS, I know something extraordinary about you: *You're alive*.

That's a tremendous gift—and it's also terrifying. The life you're living right now, the life I'm living? It's not a dress rehearsal. This is the real deal.

I'll be honest—that terrifies me as the one writing this book. The glued-together stack of paper you're holding, or the e-book, is part of your actual life. If you read it, then you won't get the time back. So I want to make the time count, yours and mine, by talking about what truly matters in life. The things that give us actual purpose and joy.

So let's take a journey together that will truly change us. Life shouldn't be about checking another book off some list. If we take the time to read something, it had better help us *live* in a new way.

Which takes us to the art of living. If we get only one shot at today, at life, how can we best live? Who should we be? How should we move through our days?

Turns out that God can show us what we're looking for.

It probably won't surprise you to hear that the Old Testament contains a ton of commandments—a whopping 613 of them!

But in the New Testament, Jesus sums up *all* of them in a single commandment: *Start by loving God with your entire being, and follow that up with loving others the way you'd like to be loved.*[1]

We see this in God's Word in a section usually called "The Greatest Commandment." Here's the version told in the Gospel of Mark:

> One of the teachers of the law came and heard them debating. Noticing that Jesus had given them a good answer, he asked him, "Of all the commandments, which is the most important?"
>
> "The most important one," answered Jesus, "is this: 'Hear, O Israel: The Lord our God, the Lord is one. Love the Lord your God with all your heart and with all your soul and with all your mind and with all your strength.' The second is this: 'Love your neighbor as yourself.' There is no commandment greater than these."
>
> "Well said, teacher," the man replied. "You are right in saying that God is one and there is no other but him. To love him with all your heart, with all your understanding and with all your strength, and to love your neighbor as yourself is more important than all burnt offerings and sacrifices."

---

[1] It has two parts, sure, but it's still a single commandment. Like how a burger and fries are a single order.

When Jesus saw that he had answered wisely, he said to him, "You are not far from the kingdom of God." And from then on no one dared ask him any more questions.[2]

The scene starts when a first-century superlawyer—not a court-of-law practitioner but an expert in the law of Moses—asks Jesus a question. And the question seems to be motivated by a pretty good instinct. (Just because he's a lawyer doesn't make him the bad guy in the story!) He notices that Jesus is giving some great answers to all the trick questions that the religious leaders are peppering him with.

So he goes for the CliffsNotes! Remember those? You'd have a test coming up about, say, *Moby Dick*, except you were only on page 13 of the book and the test was the next day. So you'd grab one of those black-and-yellow lifesavers, and an hour later you'd be set![3] That's similar to what the superlawyer is doing. He must be thinking to himself, *This teacher knows all the answers. Let's take a shortcut through all the extra stuff to see if he can answer the question that actually matters!*

It's our question too. How are we meant to live? With all the distractions and different ways of living, what's the main thing . . . and then how do we actually live it out?

Upward, Inward, Outward

As we see in Mark 12, Jesus' answer is deceptively simple: "Love the Lord your God with all your heart and with all

[2] Mark 12:28-34.
[3] If you have no idea what I'm talking about, then just substitute "Google" for "CliffsNotes."

your soul and with all your mind and with all your strength
. . . [And] love your neighbor as yourself" (verses 30–31).

Heart, soul, mind, and strength.

These make up your control center, your emotions and
will, your intellect, and your bodily abilities—pretty much
all of you!

During the time when Jesus was ministering, faithful Jews
would have recited part of the greatest commandment every
day. Some of them would even have carried it around on
index cards in their pockets or had it displayed on the lock
screens of their phones.[4] It was a big deal . . . but Jesus did
something even bigger with it.

See, there's a movement to what Jesus talks about here,
and the movement defines our lives.

Upward, inward, outward.

That's the movement described in the greatest commandment. Loving God takes us up, learning how to love ourselves
takes us in, and then we go out and love our neighbors.

And what's fascinating about Jesus' answer is that we
already live upward, inward, and outward. We can't help it.
All of us relate to God in a certain way, all of us treat ourselves a certain way, and all of us treat others a certain way.

Jesus isn't telling us to do something no human has ever
done. He's not saying, "Fly like a bird!" or "Run at the speed
of light!" or "Live life from old age to infancy!" Rather, he's
saying we need to make sure that what we're already doing,
naturally, is properly oriented.

---

4 Let the reader understand.

And why do we naturally live upward, inward, and outward? Because we were created to! But what if I told you that the needs you feel on a moment-by-moment basis are designed to draw you into a new way of living?

Let that land for a moment.

The needs you experience are invitations.

Let me explain. All of us are created with deep, profound needs, so naturally we seek to *satisfy* those needs. But unfortunately, we often seek to satisfy those needs in ways that are not only unsatisfying but also sometimes downright harmful.

We often mistake distraction for satisfaction! But a need deferred or ignored is not the same as a need fulfilled. That's why Jesus invites us into *God*-designed ways of living that will meet our needs as nothing else ever can.

But it's up to us to respond to this invitation to join him on the journey.

And don't miss the fact that God's way of living is also the way of *loving*. We don't just live in three directions—Jesus invites us to *love* in three directions.

Your deepest, most fundamental needs are invitations to love upward, inward, and outward.

And to properly respond to that invitation, we must be *intentional* about God *and* how we satisfy our needs. Instead of drifting through life or merely reacting to whatever happens to come our way, we need to figure out what's best . . . and then *do* that!

Jesus understands that we need to know what *life* is about. All of it, and not just a single season, because our seasonal answers are insufficient.

When we're teenagers, for example, we think life is all about the superlatives. We hope life grants us an identity such as *smartest, coolest, funniest, hottest, fastest*. That's how it was for me, anyway, at Cedar Ridge High. When the yearbook came out, the first section we'd flip to was the class awards. And in 1994 I was finally immortalized with my own superlative: *Most Unique*.

For a former baseball jock who was too cool (and stoned) to play senior year, this was the pinnacle. Sure, student representative to the district school board was nice. Homecoming king was sweet. Student council president didn't get me a lot of dates, but it would look good on my college applications.

But doing all those things in plaid pants and dreadlocks? Most. Unique. Ever.

What I didn't understand at the time was that I wasn't the most unique . . . and neither was anyone else!

All of us at Cedar Ridge High were just kids trying to find our place in the world. However we tried to construct that, we were still searching for meaning and purpose. We wanted to understand the art of living, but our methods were about as helpful as trying to empty a swimming pool with a coffee cup.

Too often we humans are satisfied with small definitions. Over the years I've inhabited many different roles: athlete, prep, stoner, musician, wanderer, pastor. None of those roles is *the* answer to life for me. The answer, in all those roles, is to practice the art of living.

To embody the greatest commandment and satisfy my God-given needs by living upward, inward, and outward.

Which takes us right back into the scripture we're looking at. Reread the second half. The scribe considers Jesus' answer, and he's like, "You're right, teacher. I agree! What you've said is the most important thing in the world!"

And then what Jesus *doesn't* say is, "You agree? Great, it's a done deal."

Instead he thinks about the scribe's wise answer and then says, "You are not far from the kingdom of God" (verse 34).

In other words, *outside* the Kingdom of God. Not yet living there, as an insider.

But here's the astounding part: Jesus' words are an *invitation*, not a condemnation. Jesus is saying, "Come closer. Don't be far away. Let me work in your life. You're almost home."

Taking the Next Step

So how do we bridge the distance between "not far" and "close to" Jesus?

By living in sync with the way we've been created.

God designed us completely, so he knows what it means to truly and fully live. That kind of living requires us to have a close connection to our Creator, which is the exact reason God has placed such deep needs within each of us. Without that connection, we'll still find ourselves living upward, inward, and outward—except in all the wrong ways.

That's why Jesus is so insistent we draw near. That we come closer. If we recognize how we're created, then our upward, inward, outward lives will work how they're designed to. We'll be living in step with the God who loves us deeply. God also understands the best ways for us to love him and others.

Being that close to Jesus is when life becomes not only rich and real but also transformational.

Do not miss how critical that upward movement is. Loving upward drives us to life as God intended. If we are far from the Lord, then we will always love ourselves wrongly, which will always lead us to love others wrongly as well. If we are not loving upward, nothing else works.

That's why we've got to *live* it! We're not after the "art of thinking about God a little differently." This is the art of *living*.

I love to call that art of living "Jesus spirituality"—which is ordinary people, like us, living in the deeply transformational way of Jesus.

See, information isn't enough. Not even the right information can save us by itself. We have to *act* on that information. This is the definition of wisdom, by the way—acting the right way because we have the right information.

That's why you're reading this book: because you want to integrate what you *learn* with how you *live*.

God gives us the key in the greatest commandment, but we've got to do this stuff in the right order. Imagine I invite you to my sweet cabin by the lake.[5] To start hanging out in that cabin, you need to get the key from me, pack your car, follow the GPS to the lake, and so on. There's a natural order to it.

It's the same with the greatest commandment.

We begin upward, with loving God. *The* God. God of the Old Testament, God of the New Testament. God the

---

[5] Full disclosure: I do not have a cabin of any sort. It is on my bucket list, though! But I do know how to *hike* to a lake and pitch a tent. Which is still pretty sweet.

Trinity—Father, Son, Spirit. We continue inward, with understanding our true identities in Jesus. And when we get those things right, God's Spirit sends us outward, on mission into a hurting and wonderful world.

That's how we're going to go through this book—in three movements that mirror the greatest commandment.

Movement One: Upward

This will focus on God the Father through the lens of our need for meaning, connection, intimacy, and reflection.

Movement Two: Inward

This will focus on Jesus through the lens of our need for honesty, self-control, intentionality, and humility.

Movement Three: Outward

This will focus on God's Spirit through the lens of our need for justice, self-expression, relationship, and compassion.

Discovering the art of living is a journey into the longings we were created with—and how God designed those longings to be met.

But we don't travel alone. We walk alongside the God who made us *and* our needs, stepping forward in thought *and* action, belief *and* works. Life is hard. It can be tough and unrelenting and catch us by surprise. And since we get only one shot at it, let's follow Jesus. Let's do it right. Let's live Jesus spirituality.

Let me ask you: What would your life look like if you started to love God with every part of who you are? If you based your identity on the truth of Jesus? If God's Spirit gave you the power to go out into the world, in God's name, and transform it?

If you can honestly read those questions and go, "Meh, who cares?" then you should probably give this book to someone else. You could also use it as kindling the next time you go camping or as a paperweight, or you could leave it outside for the birds to make nests with.

But if those questions stirred something in you, then let's take this journey together. Listen to what Jesus says in John 10:10: "I have come that they may have life, and have it to the full."

That's a serious statement. He's saying his life—birth, ministry, death, resurrection—exists for us. That's insane.

And insanely hopeful. The greatest commandment leads us to a life that is full, satisfying, and joyful beyond anything we can imagine.

But we only get that life by living it. Day in and day out, at street level.

And remember, the clue about how to really *live* all of this is right there in the first word of Jesus' answer to the scribe: *love*. If we're supposed to love God and love ourselves and love our neighbors, then that's *got* to be something we live out and act out. Like, no parent would say, "I can tell I love my daughter because I believe certain things about her."

That's not how love works. First John 3:18 says, "Let us not love with words or speech but with actions and in truth." Loving a kid means cleaning up vomit and holding your tongue when they're fourteen and think you're the enemy. It means combing hair and teaching Bible verses and driving to practice and doing laundry and the million other things we parents do out of love.

Jesus' invitation is getting at exactly that.

Love God, love ourselves, love others . . . with actions and in truth.

Jesus is promising us a life that is filled to overflowing with good things: joy, community, creativity, love, justice . . . pretty much the greatest hits of being alive. He says these things will permeate our lives and spill over into the world.

This is the life offered to those willing to simply respond to Jesus by taking the next step.

IF WE WANT TO LEARN the art of living, we begin where Jesus did: with the one and only God.

What we believe about God is the furthest thing from abstract. What we believe about God has very real and very practical implications for the way we live each day. It actually drives everything about us.

Here's an unfortunate current example. If you believe God wants to kill everyone who doesn't think exactly the same things you think, then you might conclude that your job is to be a holy warrior. You might even think that murdering people in the name of God is pleasing to God.

Tragically, the news is full of stories like this. It reminds me of a great quote: "You can safely assume you've created God in your own image when it turns out that God hates all the same people you do."[1]

The way we see—or don't see—God has enormous consequences in our everyday lives. It literally influences everything we think and do.

That's why we're beginning our journey with God the Father. We've got to get things right with him before we can do anything else.

And God's created us to do exactly that.

Remember, the needs deep within us are there for a reason: to make us needy! Our needs for meaning, connection, intimacy, and reflection are what point us—*drive* us, even—upward, to the only one who can truly satisfy them.

Are you ready to look up?

---

[1] Anne Lamott, *Bird by Bird: Some Instructions on Writing and Life* (New York: Anchor, 1994), 22. She attributes this to her "priest friend Tom."

1.1

meaning / worship

Problem

Who are we? Why are we here? How do we find our place in this creative, painful, beautiful thing called life? What's the main thing we should be keeping our eyes on? How can we not lose sight of that—and what's the best way to accomplish it?

I know. That's a *ton* of questions. Then again, we've got a ton of problems!

We all want to figure out life. We want to understand. We want to know what it all means. And that's where I want to begin: with the simple premise that every person longs for meaning.

Meaning is both the way we define what matters most in life and how we pursue that. Meaning is how we decide what's more or less important—and if we're lucky, it's how we know what's the *most* important thing of all.

I like how this psychologist puts it:

As human beings, we need to make meaning of our existence. Meaning gives definition to our life and our life path. This search for meaning is often challenging. How do we make sense of who we are within a world that seems out of balance with poverty, war, and famine on the one hand and tremendous privilege on the other?[1]

I mentioned in the prelude that we're going to be exploring what it means to live in three directions: upward, inward, and outward. And here in the first movement, we're looking at what it means to live upward, which might seem a strange choice.

If we're talking about the art of *living*, it seems as if inward (us) and outward (others) would be the most important. The reason we're beginning upward, though, is that the way we understand God changes everything. I believe that with all my heart.

See, what we believe (or disbelieve) about God shapes the way we think and the way we act. That's why figuring out how to live *inward* and *outward* depends on living *upward*. (If you don't believe me, stick with me at least through this chapter and the next three chapters!)

---

[1] Bob Edelstein, "The Need for Authentic Meaning: Who Am I Now? Who Do I Want to Become?" *Psychology Today*, October 15, 2012, https://www.psychologytoday.com/blog/authentic-engagement/201210/the-need-authentic-meaning.

Usually, though, we look for meaning in the next big life event, rather than in our relationship with God. *When I get to college. When I graduate. When I get my dream job. When I get married. When I have kids. When I own a house. When I get promoted.*

Those aren't bad things. The problem comes when we expect them to provide a level of meaning that they can't.

At some point we find ourselves asking why we cared so much. We might be sitting in our offices doing our "perfect" jobs, wondering why we ever expected *this* to make such a difference in our lives. There always comes a moment when the thing that was supposed to provide meaning *doesn't*, and all we can say is, "Really? That's it?"

What happens next is we figure we were chasing the wrong thing . . . so we chase the *next* thing instead.

The next job, the next relationship, the next amount of money. The "meaning treadmill" can last a lifetime—but it doesn't have to. Meaning isn't floating around somewhere, waiting to be captured. Meaning is *made*—it's what happens at the intersection of upward/inward/outward. It's what happens when what we think and believe is expressed in (or collides with) how we act. Part of the art of living is learning how to make the right meaning out of our lives.

And that depends on how we relate to God.

A lot of the time we're like fish, swimming around our little aquariums. Now I don't know much about the consciousness levels of fish, but I don't imagine a fish thinking, *Wow, my water is so interesting today! I really notice it! It seems*

7

like it's about, maybe, 0.3 degrees warmer, and it just feels so good sliding across my scales while I swim![2]

Fish are like us when it comes to meaning! The most important thing in life—God, in whom we live, move, and have our being[3]—so often escapes our attention.

Which is why I'm glad you're reading this, because I can ask you straight out: What is more important than your relationship with God?

I know that's a "pastor" kind of question, but that doesn't make it wrong! I mean, if there is a God who created and sustains everything (which I believe), then our relationship with God is ultimate.

Now here's where I'm going to take us: We all need meaning, and because ultimate meaning can only be found in our relationship with God, *worship* is what satisfies our need for meaning.

You might be like, "Okay, Fusco, not sure I buy that. That's a big jump you're making."

Yep, it is.

Promise

I want you to read the lyrics of a song I love. Kind of a golden oldie, except way older than Elvis. But it'll always be a classic . . . and it happens to be about our need for meaning.

Praise the LORD.
Sing to the LORD a new song,

---

[2] I *do* think fish are continually surprised by their little plastic plants. But I digress.
[3] Acts 17:28.

his praise in the assembly of his faithful people.
Let Israel rejoice in their Maker;
  let the people of Zion be glad in their King.
Let them praise his name with dancing
  and make music to him with timbrel and harp.
For the LORD takes delight in his people;
  he crowns the humble with victory.
Let his faithful people rejoice in this honor
  and sing for joy on their beds.

That's Psalm 149:1-5, and its theme is praise and worship—which just so happens to be the theme of the entire Bible, from Genesis to Revelation.

The Word tells the story of God and the story of people encountering God. Sometimes we honor God, and sometimes we dishonor God. It's not God who is changing across those thousands of years—it's us! Throughout every change, God continually and lovingly calls his children back to worship him.

Why? Because God deserves it, and because it is through worship we discover ourselves.

In the Ten Commandments, the *first* thing God tells us is that we should not worship anything other than God. Because he created us, God knows how prone we are to do exactly that.

We're not just tempted to worship bad stuff either. Like, it's obviously wrong to exploit the poor because we worship profit. But we even worship good stuff! We have a tendency to take good things and make them the most important things . . . which makes them bad things. Not bad because they're inherently bad, but because they take the place of God.

And worshiping *anything* that takes the place of God ruins our quest for meaning.

It's as though we're lost in the woods at night and only one person has a flashlight. If we don't make following that bobbing light our highest priority, we're not going to make it back to the parking lot. Even a good thing, like a quick water break, becomes a bad thing if it takes the place of following the leader.

Here's the thumbnail sketch of what biblical worship is. The word *worship* comes from *worth*, and the suffix *-ship*, which basically means having the "condition" or "quality" of something.[4] So if something has *worth* to us, we *worship* it, at least to a certain extent. It's possible for the same person to worship God, for example, and to worship football. Worship isn't zero-sum. But it is true that only *one* thing can be on the throne of your heart.

So if we define our whole existence by how much money we make, guess what? Money will become our life. Same with our jobs, kids, sports, and so on.

We *want* it to be possible to serve two masters. We'd each love it if we could make God our number-one priority *and* make our job our number-one priority. Can't we have it all?

Nope. Never.

That's not how life works. We are one-master creatures. The minute we elevate something to the place of honor in our hearts, we dethrone everything else.

---

[4] *Merriam-Webster Online Dictionary*, s.v. "-ship," https://www.merriam-webster.com/dictionary/ship.

It's not a matter of *if* we're worshiping. The real question is this: *Is what we're worshiping* worthy *of defining our lives?*

Because we'll only find true meaning if the object of our worship is truly worthy.

We Worship the Creator King Together

So in general worship matters—just like the specifics of *who* and *how* we worship matter. Let's go back to the first line of our song.

Praise the Lord.

Now those three words are actually a single Hebrew word. *Hallelujah. Hallel* means "praise," and *ujah* is talking about Yahweh, the Lord.[5]

The object of our praise shouldn't be random. In fact, worshiping God is the only choice that makes sense. Why? Check out this line: *Let Israel rejoice in their Maker.*

We're going to worship something, right? And there are tons of good things in our lives . . . *but none of those things* created *us*.

Only our Creator King understands the intention for which everything has been created. God doesn't just know "how to provide meaning" in some abstract sense . . . God knows how to provide *you* with the exact kind of meaning you are wired for. And God invites you to discover that through worship.

At this point, though, you might be thinking, *Well, if God's the King, then there's an awful lot of rebellion going on.*

---

[5] Ever heard a nonbeliever say, "Hallelujah"? Respond by saying, "Amen," and tell 'em you're glad they are praising God!

Why should I worship my Maker when he can't seem to control his Kingdom?

Fair question! And guess what? You're right—there's a ton of rebellion going on! Thing is, *we* are the rebels. All of us. (Unless you're perfect, in which case you probably don't need to be reading this!) And God could fix everything right now. Sure, it would destroy our free will, but he could.

But check out why he doesn't: The King's will is that no one should perish and that all should come to him.[6] Our Creator King hasn't stamped down humanity's rebellion against his royal authority because he wants us to be saved! If Jesus had come back twenty years ago, *I would never have known him.* And that happens every day, all around the world.

That's the kind of king I love serving. The kind of king I will give my life for if needed. And the one I want to worship.

The best part is that when I worship, I get to stand beside my brothers and sisters in a worshiping *community*. Theologians call this *corporate* worship, which is just a fancy way of saying that all the parts of Christ's body—all of *us*—come together for one purpose.[7]

Worshiping together isn't *one* way to worship. It's *the* way to worship.

Now I'm not saying it's impossible to worship alone. We worship in our cars and in cubicles and in solitary confinement. But those instances of worship connect us with our Creator King, and with Jesus, and are meant to propel us

---

[6] 2 Peter 3:8-9.

[7] The word *corporate* comes from *corpus*. As in *corpse*. But our corporate worship makes our dead bodies come alive, praise God (Ephesians 2:5).

back together to give thanks and learn and sing. In our sinful world, it isn't always possible to worship together in community. But corporate worship is part of God's design. Read Psalm 149:1 again: "Sing to the LORD a new song, his praise *in the assembly of his faithful people*" (emphasis added).

This is one of the reasons I believe faithful, orthodox Christianity is such a challenge in the twenty-first-century West.

Think about it. Our culture is *all* about the individual. About *me*. My relationship with God, my experience at church, my family, my money, my hobbies. The list goes on and on. This is at the DNA level for most of us. But the interesting thing is that all through the Bible, it's about community. About us and we and everyone. From Genesis 1:26 ("Let us make [humans] in our image . . .) to Deuteronomy 6:4 ("Hear, O Israel: the LORD our God") to Jesus ("Our Father . . . ") to the Epistles (1 Corinthians 12 and 13) to our ultimate home (Revelation).

God saves us *from* our sins and places us *into* a worshiping community. (More on that later in chapter 3.3.)

That's where we make the kind of meaning that will last a lifetime—and beyond.

We Worship in the Spirit and in Truth

Our need for meaning takes us to John 4, which tells the story of Jesus talking to someone scholars refer to as "the woman at the well."[8] She was a Samaritan, which according to Jesus' culture

---

[8] There's a complex theological reason for this terminology: She was a woman . . . and she was at a well.

meant he should have hated her. And she was a multidivorcée living with her latest boyfriend, while he was an upstanding single man. Meaning he should have steered clear.

Before we continue, let that sink in for a sec: Jesus wasn't just polite to people who crossed his path . . . he *sought out* people he was supposed to avoid!

Here's what Jesus says to her in verse 24: "God is spirit, and his worshipers must worship in the Spirit and in truth."

Our need for meaning is satisfied when we worship both in the Spirit and in truth. It's like two sides of one coin. Better yet, it's like looking at something with both eyes open. Using both eyes is what gives us 3-D vision and allows us to, for example, catch a baseball before it smacks us in the head. With only one eye open, what we see is flattened and limited.

Unfortunately, when it comes to worship, we're *really* good at focusing on either the Spirit *or* the truth.

Let's start with the Spirit. No matter what our backgrounds or denominations—or even personal preferences— *we need to worship God expressively*, in the Spirit. Psalm 149:3 shows us why. I love this: "Make music to him with timbrel and harp." Whoever wrote this psalm didn't know about the electric bass, obviously, but if they did? *Make music to him with drums and bass!*

You might be saying to yourself, "Bro, I just like to keep it low-key and not pretend to be all emotional about everything."

If you're saying that, don't freak out.[9] We're not talking about your eternal salvation or anything.

---

9 Or if you prefer the King James Version, "Freakest thou not!"

At the same time, however, I hope to show you a better way! Because when it comes to worship, some of us are too cool for school, and that completely misses God's design for us.

Here's an example. I love being a parent. And I love my son, Obadiah. Right now he's at that age where he's too cool to show affection for me in public. After a recent soccer game, I was going to wrap him up in a big hug. But he knew that, so he tried to go ninja on me and duck under the hug. Except *I* knew that *he* knew, and I snagged him anyway and said, "So now you're too cool for me to put my arms around you?"

"No."

"Then give Daddy a kiss. Come on, buddy . . . what's going to happen if your friends see me kiss you?"

Pray for my son. I'm probably messing him up something good! Thing is, he loves me a ton. When we're in the van or at home, he's all about the hugs and chitchat and fist bumps and camaraderie. It's just that when we're in public, he has a different standard. Which is, basically, *act like you don't know me*.

If that's the way you worship, you're doing it wrong. I'm just gonna tell you straight out, okay, and pray that you keep reading!

Sometimes we're like (read this in your *least* expressive voice), "Yep, uh-huh, praise God. Mmm-hmm. Praise, praise, praise . . . are we done praising yet?"

But God isn't just worthy of worship—God is worthy of *passionate* worship.

One of my favorite examples of this comes from 2 Samuel 6. You'll have to read it yourself, but the main idea is that King David, who's the most powerful person in the whole land, gets so excited by worshiping God that he dances "with all his might" (verse 14). With a band, at a public parade. And did I mention he was in his underwear?

We probably shouldn't show up to church next week in our tighty-whities, but we should allow the Spirit of God to move us and inspire us, even if it's uncomfortable at first.

Okay, now that I've got us dancing in our underwear and praising God . . . let's take a little Gatorade break and read the Word again. It's time to look at how to worship in truth.

The truth—about God, about us, about our world—causes us to be humble. And humility causes us to seek out the truth, because we know we need it. If you were about to die of kidney failure and a stranger appeared out of nowhere to give you their kidney, you wouldn't be like, "Um, thanks."

You'd be more like, "Oh my goodness! Sorry for crying, and thank you infinity times infinity!"

When our worship highlights the truth of what God has done for us in Christ, we are humbled by that truth and then driven to even deeper worship.

And our need for meaning is truly satisfied.

Worshiping in the Spirit *and* in truth isn't rocket science. We want to be followers of Jesus who avoid spiritual pitfalls, right? So on the one hand, we don't want to be Bible thumpers who beat everyone up with *truth truth truth*. If we aren't animated by the Spirit, the Bible becomes just a list of rules to judge everyone else by. On the other hand, we don't want to be experience junkies, always chasing the next "spiritual" moment that gives us the shivers.

God has taken us from a life of rebellion and given us a

place in his family, and that's where meaning surrounds us and motivates us. We become passionate about the art of living because of who God is and what God has done, not the other way around.

We don't come to God and say, "Yep, of course you saved me—I deserved it!" Instead we cry out, "God, I can't believe you saved me. *Me*, of all people!"

We ask God, "How can I ever thank you? How can I share what you've done?"

The answer to the first question is worship.

And the answer to the *second* question is worship!

Art-of-living worship. Our need for meaning always leads to worship—and worshiping our Creator makes the only kind of meaning that will satisfy us.

We Worship with Joy

I love how our psalm culminates in *joy*.

Joy is an easy sell because *everybody* wants it. But let me take us on a super quick detour, because we actually find joy somewhere unexpected.

In Romans 12:1, the apostle Paul says, "Therefore, I urge you, brothers and sisters, in view of God's mercy, to offer your bodies as a living sacrifice, holy and pleasing to God—this is your true and proper worship." He's saying *we* do this because of what *God* has already done for us. When you and I worship as people who are humbly saved, we find the art of living.

Richard Foster says it this way: "As worship begins in holy expectancy, it ends in holy obedience."[10]

---

[10] Richard J. Foster, *Celebration of Discipline: The Path to Spiritual Growth* (New York: HarperCollins, 1998), 173.

Be honest: Does holy obedience sound boring and joyless?

It's the opposite! Holy obedience is worshiping with a community of friends. It's being on mission together. It's responding with gratefulness to God. And when we declare the worth of God with our lives, God shares his joy with us.

Our God is the most joyful person in the universe—and his joy subverts our expectations about what joy is. God's joy does not depend on or ensure that everything works out perfectly. It isn't circumstantial. God's joy is the disposition of a heart that knows "it is well with my soul" because God is God. This is the joy he shares with us when we come to him with worship.

The thing about living with *God's* joy, rather than our own, is that our souls can rest in God even when our life circumstances push us to fear or freak out. When I watch how followers of Jesus respond to suffering with joy, though, I see the only evidence I need that God is who God says.

When it comes to joy in hard circumstances, it's a blessing and a curse to be a pastor. I see people in their greatest moments and in their worst moments. If the meaning we crave is found in worship, that meaning has got to make sense throughout all of life. *All* of life, even the parts that feel like they'll break us, or else it's counterfeit meaning.

Life isn't pretty or neat. Life can hurt. Bad. I know too many people who have been absolutely crushed by pain. But when I see those very people stand up in the assembly of believers, hand over shattered heart, and worship with joy?

Apart from God being God and delivering on *every single promise*, it makes no sense.

And when I see God's joy in action, being lived out, it drives *me* to worship with joy. To worship the only one who can satisfy my need for meaning in this painful, beautiful life.

See how that works? We find true meaning when we worship God, together, with joy, in all of life.

Any lasting meaning must be built on our relationship with the one who means everything. Unless we worship the true and living God, all our attempts at worship will leave us unsatisfied, unfulfilled, and grasping at the air.

They'll leave us searching for meaning and never finding it.

Maybe you're saying, "I don't know if you're on target, Fusco. I can be happy in lots of ways. I can find meaning in lots of things."

You're right. We *can* find meaning in lots of things.

But there is only one place to find ultimate, perfect, loving, redemptive, promise-in-the-middle-of-pain, eternal meaning. And our only response when we find it is to worship.

Practice

Since worship is the way we live our lives—every day and not just Sunday—we practice it every waking moment. Here's a reminder of how we can get started.

Worship means living toward whatever we value most.

 Do you value God more than anything else? How can you tell? Would others be able to say that about you?

 Take a moment this week to look at how you spend your

time and energy. Consider what your choices say about what you value. Decide if you'd like to make any changes to your schedule or habits or lifestyle in order to place more value on God.

God intends for you to worship expressively, truthfully, and in community.

⬆ Are you part of a church body? Do you make the Bible a regular part of your life? Are you willing to let your hair down and worship with passion and expression?

⬆ Thank someone in your church body for inspiring you or teaching you. Keep a Bible on the front seat of your car, and read *one* verse whenever you park your car. List some worship practices that part of you wishes you could do, such as raising your hands or dancing or singing at the top of your lungs.

Unshakable joy is the outcome of true worship.

⬆ Is your happiness dependent on your circumstances, or do you have a joy grounded in the truth of who God is, what God has done, and what God has promised?

⬆ Thank God for being at your side during the most painful times of your life. Pray for a friend or family member who is walking through "the valley of the shadow of death."[11]

---

[11] Psalm 23:4, ESV.

1.2

connection / prayer

Problem

I'm old enough to look back and notice patterns in my life, and one I've thought about lately is that I've never *not* been part of a tribe. I've always been connected with others. Not because I intentionally make a list of priorities or anything like that. It just happens to me, automatically. Which, as an extrovert, feels perfect.

It all goes back to my childhood. I talk a ton about my family in my previous book, *Honestly*, but if this is your first time with me, I'll give you a quick introduction. Picture the biggest, loudest, most stereotypical Italian family imaginable.[1] Now make sure that family lives in New Jersey! Not

---

[1] Also, if you don't know me, picture a really handsome and fit dude . . . basically Ryan Gosling but with dreadlocks.

a week went by without a houseful of family members and close friends, eating and drinking and talking about every topic under the sun. The noise of our laughter terrified the neighborhood cats. And my tribe didn't stop there—I had my baseball teams, my crew of buddies, and my coworkers.

So when I moved to college, constant connection was my normal. In no time at all I was part of new tribes: dorm life, parties, my band. College was friends, friends, and more friends. There was always something to do and someone to hang out with.

After college it was more of the same. As a professional musician, I naturally moved into a big house with a bunch of other musicians. We ate, drank, and lived music. We even slept music, since no matter what time of day or night it was, there was always someone trying to figure out some music and always someone trying to catch some z's. I was surrounded by people 24-7, just as I'd always been. Just as I wanted to be.

It wasn't until I hit the ripe old age of twenty-two that the following question hit me: *How come I still feel lonely sometimes?*

I had a great family, great friends, a great band . . . yet I sensed something was missing. It was like I felt connected, but not connected *enough*. Or I felt connected, but not to the right thing. Whatever the reason, loneliness began to gnaw at me like a mouse going to work on a baseboard. The hole grew imperceptibly, but it grew steadily.

Finally, I had to be honest and ask myself, *If two decades of constant connection aren't the solution to my need for connection . . . what is?*

All of us are designed to be connected to something bigger

than ourselves, but we often don't know what that is. We can't stay disconnected, though, so we hope for the best and look for connection in whatever we can. We look to nature or romantic relationships or financial gurus or work. We look to gardening clubs or our kids or social networking or online games.[2] We humans can't resist the impulse to come together with others, somewhere, somehow.

But to borrow a phrase from Johnny Lee, we're looking for connection in all the wrong places.[3] Or at least incomplete places. Those things I mention might not be wrong, but they're insufficient. Something is still missing.

That's how we get ourselves into trouble. Since we'd rather be connected to something, rather than nothing, we're willing to try almost anything.

Promise

This might sound counterintuitive, but I believe our need for connection in general is truly satisfied only when we are connected specifically to God. And that requires prayer.

Because of how we've been designed, a private relationship is what meets our longing to be connected. Because the longing inside our longing is actually a need for *spiritual connection*. That need is part of what makes us human. And it's more than just a natural need: It's a God-given need.

There are two reasons for that. One, God knows our lives

---

[2] Recently (yet another) online game closed its virtual doors for good, and people freaked out, almost as if they were losing their *selves*. That's less a sad commentary on them than it is a sad commentary on *us*: the friends and family members and neighbors whose actions or lack of actions made it seem as if the only way these gamers could find a connection was sitting alone in a room.

[3] Johnny Lee, "Lookin' for Love," Full Moon, 1980.

will be more fulfilling, more filled with love, more exciting and challenging, if we live them alongside other people. And two, God knows that living alongside other people, in community, *is the best way to point us to our need for* spiritual *connection.*

When I was twenty-one, that sense of loneliness gnawing at me was God's way of getting my attention. God was starting to let me know that a better kind of connection was waiting for me. Not a connection that made my human connections obsolete or wrong. It was the opposite. What I was missing was true spiritual connection, and that gift would do more than connect me with my Creator.

It would also deepen and strengthen my *existing* connections.

Prayer is the discipline that satisfies our need for spiritual connection. And I've never met *anyone* who says, "You know, I actually pray *plenty* . . . way too much, in fact!"

See the link? We don't feel connected enough because we don't pray enough.

I've heard it said you can tell how popular a church is by how many people come on Sunday, how popular a pastor is by how many people come to the midweek Bible study, and how popular Jesus is by how many people come to the prayer meeting. Recently at church we had a night of prayer and worship, and when people realized there wasn't going to be a sermon, you know what happened? The crowd thinned out. A lot.

Without getting all judgy, here's what I think that tells us: *We don't understand that prayer is God's primary way to meet our need for connection.*

Billy Graham was once asked what he'd do differently

if he could live his life over again, and he answered that he would pray more.[4] That's how many of us feel. We'd like to pray more, and we know we *should* pray more.

But prayer is so difficult.

It's way easier to call up a friend or text someone or go on Facebook. Connect, connect, connect. Except it's like trying to take a shower one drip at a time: We've got the right *idea*, but the wrong execution.

The Bible makes very clear promises about prayer, however. For example, take Psalm 145:18:

> The LORD is near to all who call on him,
>   to all who call on him in truth.

Our need for connection can absolutely be met. We can feel completely satisfied in God. The catch is, we've got to go about it in the right way.[5]

The Pattern of Prayer

Exactly zero of you will be surprised that I'm going to talk about the Lord's Prayer in a chapter about prayer. My goal is to be quick and interesting and relevant, though, so let's dive into what the Bible promises about prayer.

Remember, as we look at the art of living, what we're trying to do is find the *way to live* that's hiding beneath the *way we're living*.

---

4 "Billy Graham Interview: If You Want to Do Things Over Again, Would You Do It Differently?," YouTube video, 2:27, posted by Albrecht Wattimury, March 14, 2013, https://www.youtube.com /watch?v=2dIuWwQAOTo.

5 I didn't invent the following elements of pattern, persistence, and principle. I stole a bit from Warren Wiersbe, discovered some on Google, and found a few that I'd written in the margin of my Bible—I'll credit those to my former pastor, John Henry Corcoran.

We live upward, we live inward, and we live outward—simultaneously. We get that from Jesus' greatest commandment. And while it's tempting to focus inward (on ourselves) or outward (on what everyone else needs), we must begin upward. That's the foundation. That's what drives everything else.

With that in mind, let's start with our passage from Matthew, where Jesus teaches his disciples about prayer. Luke records a version of it as well, but Matthew's is more familiar:

This, then, is how you should pray:

"Our Father in heaven,
hallowed be your name,
your kingdom come,
your will be done,
    on earth as it is in heaven.
Give us today our daily bread.
And forgive us our debts,
    as we also have forgiven our debtors.
And lead us not into temptation,
    but deliver us from the evil one."[6]

I like to call this the model prayer rather than the Lord's Prayer. That's what it is: a model, or a pattern, for how we ought to pray. (Plus, the *Lord's* prayer is really in John 17, just before he is betrayed by Judas, arrested, and later crucified.)

---

[6] Matthew 6:9-13.

Jesus takes his friends through a short prayer that never-theless talks about pretty much everything in the universe: God's glory, human needs—from physical to spiritual to emotional—the communities we live in, and the struggle against evil.

To avoid writing an entire book about this prayer, I'm going to confine myself to a few highlights.

Hallowed is a word we don't use much anymore, but it simply means "special" and "significant" and "set apart." And because the name of a person is a shortcut for that person's entire being—think of having a "good name" or "ruining a good name"—we know right off that the one we're praying to is uniquely special.

That gets our foundation—our upward view—cor-rect. And it's what connects God's name with God's reign. When we invite God's Kingdom and God's will, we're talk-ing about the reign of a King. When was the last time you said, "God, I want your Kingdom to come into my life"? Because that's exactly the way God's Kingdom comes: when God reigns and God's will is done in and through your life. God's Kingdom comes through people like you and me. Is your life a place where the division between heaven and earth is so thin that God's grace and love can enter the world through you?

Next we're invited to name our needs, and it's really interesting how Jesus speaks about those needs as "our daily bread." Someone once said God promises to provide for our needs, not our greeds. Too often we confuse what we need with what we want, and our culture doesn't make it any easier on us—we *need* a new television or *need* faster Internet.

But every so often we get a fresh perspective on the difference between needs and wants. Recently my family and I had an issue with our kitchen, and the whole thing got ripped out. We quickly realized how many things we take for granted in our lives. It was like, "How are we going to survive without ice-cold filtered water on tap and without a dishwasher?"

I joke, except not really. We were able to buy a hot plate and move the fridge to the garage and get along quite nicely. (We also ate more take-out burritos, which was a win for me.) But the experience gave us a dose of perspective. We realized how ridiculously comfortable we are, almost all the time. Instead of complaining about the upheaval of an unplanned kitchen remodel, we were grateful we *had* a kitchen. And a house. And electricity and running water.

This kind of thing is hard for us Westerners. We want our daily bread, *and* we want our long-term bread! We want to hit our retirement numbers and be comfortable and check off everything on our bucket lists. Not that these things are bad or wrong. They aren't. But Jesus gives us a much-needed perspective check.

Bread isn't the only thing we need every day. It may not even be the most important thing. Immediately following the request for physical sustenance is a request for forgiveness. The Christian message is that God says to us, "You owe me a debt because your rebellion has severed our relationship. Since you can't pay that debt—and because I love you so much—I'm going to send my Son to satisfy that debt for

you and restore our relationship." And just as we need forgiveness from God, we need forgiveness from other people
we've hurt. Plus, we need to forgive them. What's amazing
about being connected to God is that as we receive forgiveness, we become able to truly forgive others who have hurt
us and humble ourselves to ask others to forgive us.

God being glorified, God's Kingdom coming, needs
being met, forgiveness happening . . . that's exactly the sort
of stuff Satan is dead set on stopping. In our day and age, we
don't like to talk about the devil. It seems primitive, right?
And Satan is good with that. In fact, he prefers that we either
ignore him or be obsessed with him.[7] But Satan is definitely
real. We can't see him—just like we can't see gravity—but his
effects are just as observable, and he's just as real.

And isn't it weird we make physical proof the standard for
believing in his existence, given that we believe in an unseen
God? There are lots of things we believe without physical
evidence. I don't have any physical evidence that proves my
mother loved me when she was alive. But I know it beyond
the hint of a shadow of a doubt. Not everything that is true
is evidentiary. Our hesitancy to admit Satan is real probably
has more to do with not wanting to look foolish or backward
in our culture.

But Satan is real. And Jesus tells us to pray for deliverance.

So the Lord's Prayer, or Jesus' model prayer, gives us a
pattern. It isn't a formula. It's not the only way to pray. But

---

7 "There are two equal and opposite errors into which our race can fall about the devils. One is to
disbelieve in their existence. The other is to believe, and to feel an excessive and unhealthy interest in
them. They themselves are equally pleased by both errors and hail a materialist or a magician with the
same delight." C. S. Lewis, *The Screwtape Letters* (New York: Harper Collins, 1996), ix.

it does give us ways to think about the *who* and the *what* of prayer.

The Persistence of Prayer

Now let's look at the *when*, because prayer requires persistence.

In the Luke passage, immediately after teaching the disciples to pray, Jesus says this:

> Suppose you have a friend, and you go to him at midnight and say, "Friend, lend me three loaves of bread; a friend of mine on a journey has come to me, and I have no food to offer him." And suppose the one inside answers, "Don't bother me. The door is already locked, and my children and I are in bed. I can't get up and give you anything." I tell you, even though he will not get up and give you the bread because of friendship, yet because of your shameless audacity he will surely get up and give you as much as you need.[8]

That's an amazing and frightening way to think about prayer: approaching God with shameless audacity!

This is one of the stories Jesus tells that needs a bit of unpacking because most of us don't get visits from friends in the middle of the night. Back then, however, it was pretty common. If you had a long journey, you might start at dusk in order to avoid traveling while it was hot enough to crisp a camel. So if you made good time, you might show up while

---

[8] Luke 11:5-8.

it was still night. But what about the next part, where the neighbor is like, "Why should I care about your little bread situation—me and my whole family are in bed already!"?

This makes me think of the insanity of the "family bed."

The other night my daughter Maranatha tapped me on the shoulder in the middle of the night. "Dad, I had a bad dream."

I looked at my wife, who looked right back at me.

"Okay, baby, you can climb in with us," I said.

She snuggled in, and both she and my wife fell asleep a few minutes later. Which was sweet for a grand total of thirty seconds. Because once Maranatha was actually *asleep*, she turned diagonal, stuck her icy cold feet on my shins, and began to mutter. I loved it—and absolutely *didn't* love it.

I picked her up like a sack of potatoes and carried her back to bed. She didn't wake up, praise God, and neither did my wife.

In the story Jesus tells, the whole family is in the same room, and the doors to that room—which were the doors to the house—were shut and locked. So the neighbor in our parable was basically saying, "Man, if I open the door to get you your bread, then everyone in my house, including my kids, are gonna wake up . . . and I have a business meeting in the morning!"

That's why Jesus tells us to be persistent. Tenacious. Bold. Because he wants us to be the kind of people who don't give up on something—or on him.

Most of us, when we pray about something that doesn't

happen, we stop praying. And that's *exactly* why God doesn't usually answer our requests immediately. We know God isn't a cosmic vending machine, but a lot of times we *act* like he is. God knows our hearts and our natures, and he wants us to learn to seek after his heart. He wants us to become like Jesus, over time.

And just like that, we're back at the bull's-eye: We need connection.

The spiritual connection we long for doesn't come from getting everything we want the second we want it. Rather, it happens as we grow in our relationship with God. The Bible uses a picture for that, borrowed from farming. Jesus says, "Abide in me. . . . for apart from me you can do nothing."[9]

Connection takes persistence. It takes patience and grit and even shameless audacity! But if our prayers have those qualities, we will deepen our relationship with God. Continually seeking God will continually shape us. We'll be searching the Bible and claiming promise after promise and praying with other believers. We'll be listening. And all the while, we'll be looking more like Jesus . . . and becoming more satisfied with our spiritual connection.

Not to mention, the Bible tells us God's timing is different from ours. Persistence is how we sync God's time with our time.

The Principle of Prayer

We have a pattern, and we know we need to be persistent. Finally, let's look at the principle of prayer. A principle is

---

9 John 15:4-5, ESV.

something true at the base layer, like a foundation strong enough to build everything else on. When it comes to prayer, the foundational principle is that God is good—and wants to give us what we need.

Jesus' teaching about prayer in Luke closes with this:

So I say to you: Ask and it will be given to you; seek and you will find; knock and the door will be opened to you. For everyone who asks receives; the one who seeks finds; and to the one who knocks, the door will be opened.

Which of you fathers, if your son asks for a fish, will give him a snake instead? Or if he asks for an egg, will give him a scorpion? If you then, though you are evil, know how to give good gifts to your children, how much more will your Father in heaven give the Holy Spirit to those who ask him![10]

Ask, seek, and knock is what it all comes down to. Greek scholars tell us these words are ongoing and perpetual. Persistent, in other words. We keep on asking and seeking and knocking, over and over and over. Why?

Because we'll receive what we're searching for and our needs will be met. If we continue to pray, we'll be connected to God. God *will* do this. It's certain—as certain as the fact that we, despite being screwups, still generally know how to treat our kids well. We feed them when they're hungry, for

---

[10] Luke 11:9-13.

example. Which means we meet their needs. And if we can do that, God can do that a kajillion times over.

We have a good God who loves us as a Father and who wants to bring blessings into our lives. God wants to give us the things that will bring blessings into the world. And because God's greatest blessing is himself, we're encouraged to ask and keep on asking! The true motivation for prayer is our need for God. The true focus of prayer is God. The true outcome of prayer is a relationship with God.

We pray for things we *think* we need. But if our prayers are patterned after Jesus' model prayer, and if our prayers are persistent, and if we never forget the underlying principle of prayer, then God gives us what we *actually* need.

We discover that God is always good and that we are connected to him. Which is, in a way, the answer to every prayer we can ever pray.

God is real. God is here. And prayer is the way we connect with God.

You and I can definitely choose not to pray, even if we're Christians! But we'll always have that need, that longing, for connection. And if God isn't meeting that need for us, we're going to look for connection in all the wrong places.

How we live upward determines how we live inward and outward. There's simply too much at stake to *not* be people of prayer.

Practice

I'm trying to learn the art of living, right along with you. And as someone living in the mess, I can agree with you about this: *One of the reasons we struggle with prayer is that there isn't only one right way to do it!*

We want there to be a single, foolproof "way to pray," but there isn't. Not even the model prayer Jesus taught us is the *only* way to pray. And you probably know why by this point in the chapter: because God wants a relationship with us, and relationships go through periods of growth and change.

So I want to encourage you: If you're a praying person, you're going to practice many ways of praying over time. You'll try different things. You'll respond to seasons in your life. You'll allow God's presence and God's Word to guide and shape your practice over time. Which is why the most important *practical* thing I can say about prayer is a single word: *experiment.*

You can pray aloud, and you can pray silently. You can pray publicly or in private. You can pray casually and conversationally, or you can pray formally. You can write a letter to God. You can pray along with a prayer that someone else has already written. You can pray Scripture. You can pray while you walk or stand or kneel or run or drive. You can pray in an instant or pray for hours.

Don't get stuck. Don't blindly copy what works for someone else.

Listen to your Creator, and respond.

Just as there are different ways to pray, there are different things to pray about. Since we can pray about anything, we can sometimes feel paralyzed by choice. One tip for praying in different categories is to use an acronym, such as PRAY:

Praise
Repent
Ask for others
Ask for **Y**ourself

It's not important—at *all*—that we follow the PRAY pattern each time. It is important, however, that we remember prayer is a conversation about real things with a real Person. Would you ever have a friendship in which the *only* thing you ever talked about was what you needed?

So let's confess and adore and intercede and rest and give thanks and plead and question and claim promises and everything else we do in a real relationship.

However we pray, and whatever we pray, the key is that we remember we're actually connecting with God—a miraculous relationship made possible by the work of Jesus and the power of the Spirit.

Take some time this week to think about your prayer life.

- How often do you usually pray each week, and in what circumstances?
- Is there a kind of prayer you're most comfortable with? What kinds of prayer make you uncomfortable?
- What can you learn from the Lord's model prayer?
- What are the areas of life where you doubt the goodness of God?
- Where can you start to grow in prayer?

Remember, prayer is "the deepest and highest work of the human spirit. Real prayer is life creating and life changing."[11]

Just as you were born with a need for true connection, you were also born with the solution. In prayer you will be connected to the one perfect source of goodness and growth.

---

[11] Richard Foster, "The Main Business of Life," in *The Contemporaries Meet the Classics on Prayer*, comp. Leonard Allen (West Monroe, LA: Howard, 2003), 16.

1.3

↑ ↙ ↗

intimacy / solitude

Problem

I don't think it's an oversimplification to say that we humans are defined by our need for relationships.

That might be why so many of the needs we talk about in this book are relational. The art of living—upward, inward, outward—always involves relationships. Except as we saw in the last chapter, it's not *merely* "a relationship" we need. Our need for relationship surfaces other, deeper needs, such as our need for prayer, self-expression, and compassion. (Keep reading, in other words!)

The hopeful news is God promises that our needs can be met, which makes sense, because God created us with those needs in the first place. We're hardwired for relationships, but what God *doesn't* promise is that this need will be met automatically. It actually takes work, but it's worth it because the more our needs are met by God, the healthier and happier we'll be.

Okay, now let's get intimate. Because I'm going to show you how one of our deepest, most obvious needs—the need for intimacy—is met. Not by other people but by God. And not by words but by stillness and silence and rest.

I know, it sounds crazy, but hang in there. Let me show you how it works.

As a culture, we've taken the idea of intimacy and reduced it to one, maybe two, elements. Sex, for sure, and maybe closeness. Those can be part of intimacy, but they don't tell the whole story. It's like a symphony in which we ignore all the instruments except two.

If we stop to think about intimacy, though, we can come up with a much better definition.

The best relationships we've been in—and maybe are still in—are characterized by honesty and trust. We feel like we can be our true selves in an intimate relationship. Intimacy means we can let our guard down. When we aren't trying to defend ourselves or project a certain image, we can relax. We can be known. We're able to experience the full range of emotions and experiences and not just the "safe" ones we allow acquaintances to see. We share our inner world with our most intimate friends, and we get to enjoy theirs. It's not just inner worlds, either: We live life together.

But even with that expanded understanding of intimacy,

our need can't be fully met by other people. It doesn't matter how many awesome coworkers we have. It doesn't matter how real and honest and supportive our Facebook feed can seem. It doesn't matter if we have the best neighbors on the planet.

It doesn't even matter if we're married or have a lifelong best friend.

Those things are all good . . . but there's one more level of intimacy that can be met only by God.

Which isn't to say that our most intimate human relationships are somehow pointless. They very much have a point—part of which is to drive us even closer to Christ. Here's a quick example.

Recently I was watching our youngest daughter sleep. (If that sounds kinda creepy, wait until you have kids!) So I'm looking at her sleep, and she looks so peaceful and beautiful, and all of a sudden she opens her eyes. Now if she'd been a baby, I would've been in big trouble for waking her up, but she was a year and a half, and the best thing happened: The minute our eyes locked on each other, she smiled. And I smiled back. There was this moment beyond words in which we were just sharing the sweetness of loving each other. She was loving her big, hairy daddy, and I was just adoring my amazing daughter. It was an intimacy beyond words.

Isn't that beautiful? And check this out: Even though my daughter can't satisfy my deepest need for intimacy, our relationship inspires me and points me to live *upward*, connected to God. Our wordless intimacy, our trusting stillness, points me to my heavenly Father.

Psalm 46:10 says,

Be still, and know that I am God;
    I will be exalted among the nations,
    I will be exalted in the earth.

When was the last time you were totally and *intimately* silent? Even now, if you put down this book, chances are sky-high it won't be silent. You'll hear your fan or heater, or kids if you're at home. You'll hear the buzz of conversation in the coffee shop.

But as we're about to see, it's in silence we meet God . . . and in silence God meets our need for intimacy.

Promise

Be still. That's what God tells us. Be still and *know*. Isn't that fascinating?

God doesn't say, "Be still and *hope* that I am God." Or "Be still and try to convince yourself that I am God."

In stillness we *know* God is God.

And that's the knowledge that leads to true intimacy.

God's Word shows us over and over that God is found in stillness.

Us, though? We're people who live with a near total lack of silence, a near total lack of stillness and solitude and rest. So is it any wonder that we struggle to know that God is God?

Consider how different Jesus' life was from our connected, hectic, frantic lives. This is a man who spent forty days alone in the wilderness. His phone didn't get any reception, of course, and neither did his tablet.[1]

In all seriousness, Jesus spent a ton of time alone, in silence. A quick but not exhaustive list of times he sought out stillness: forty days in the desert,[2] after hearing about his friend John the Baptist being killed,[3] after miraculously feeding thousands,[4] after healing many individuals,[5] and before he was arrested.[6] He sometimes avoided—or even ran from—crowds. He spent nights outside by himself. He rose before dawn. Over and over he sought solitude.

Why? Because that was where he found his Father. That's where he met God.

If Jesus needed to seek solitude and stillness and silence, then we *definitely* do. I don't care how hectic life in the ancient Near East was, things are way crazier for us.[7]

And Jesus wasn't the only person in the Bible to seek out quietude. Paul went into the Arabian wilderness. Moses tended sheep for years in the desert before returning to Pharaoh's court. Gideon met the Lord while he was alone in a cave. Jacob slept outside by a stream at Bethel with a rock pillow. When we read our Bibles, we see that God seems to communicate most clearly in times of solitude and stillness.

It's still that way today.

Recently a man at church shared this story with me. He

---

[1] Lest there be *any* confusion on this point, I jest. Jesus did not have a tablet. I mean, where would he even have plugged it in?
[2] Matthew 4:1-11.
[3] Matthew 14:13.
[4] Matthew 14:23.
[5] Luke 5:16.
[6] Matthew 26:36-46.
[7] They had their own challenges, of course. Like no modern dental care or John Coltrane albums.

had been on a hunting trip by himself, and on that Sunday morning he climbed to the top of a nearby peak. He wanted to be alone, in silence. What he didn't know was that at the same time, his wife was at church, praying for him.

Know what happened on that mountaintop? He met God in a new and special way. God spoke to him about his life and his marriage. The very things his wife was praying for, the true and living God was speaking to him. And he wept and worshiped. He told me he took Communion up there, with trail mix and his canteen.

In that mountaintop stillness, he *knew* God was God. That intimacy changed him.

Gentle Whisper

Okay, let's open God's Word. We're going to look at several passages as we explore how our need for intimacy is answered by God's stillness. We'll begin with 1 Kings 19:11-13. The prophet Elijah is on the run from a bunch of royal soldiers who are trying to kill him. (Understandably, since he'd just publicly embarrassed the king and slaughtered all the king's pet soothsayers.) When Elijah has more or less given up all hope and he wants to die, check out what happens:

> The LORD said, "Go out and stand on the mountain in the presence of the LORD, for the LORD is about to pass by."
>
> Then a great and powerful wind tore the mountains apart and shattered the rocks before the LORD, but the LORD was not in the wind. After the

wind there was an earthquake, but the LORD was not in the earthquake. After the earthquake came a fire, but the LORD was not in the fire. And after the fire came a *gentle whisper*. When Elijah heard it, he pulled his cloak over his face and went out and stood at the mouth of the cave. [Emphasis added.]

If you've hung around church before, there's a good chance you've heard someone talk about the "still small voice" of God. This is the passage it comes from. However we translate it, the emphasis is on God upending our expectations about where he can be found.

We simply cannot learn the art of living if we are unable to find personal places of stillness, because it is only in that stillness that we can hear the whisper of God.

By the way, this stillness and silence we're talking about has nothing to do with whether we're introverts or extroverts. If you're an introvert, you've been nodding along with some of what I'm saying. Like, *I totally relate to hearing from God in the silence—preach it!* But this intimate solitude is for everyone who wants to follow Jesus. With me being an extrovert, I need to hear this message repeatedly. My wife will sometimes look for me after the kids are in bed, and she'll find me downstairs on the couch. I'll have the TV on an old episode of *Criminal Minds*, music playing in the background, and a book open on my Kindle—and I'm also playing bass. The more noise and sound, the better.

Stillness is not my sweet spot.

But as much as I realize that doing everything at once

brings me a certain amount of happiness, and as much as I enjoy multi-multitasking, I also realize that those are rarely the times I hear the voice of God.

We—introverts and extroverts alike—are good at seeking intimacy in almost every place *except* the still, small voice of God. That's what we've got to tune into, rather than the wind, the earthquake, and the fire.

Sabbath: Part One

Did you know God uses a different term for stillness than we do?

He calls it *Sabbath*.

Sabbath is God's way of talking about stillness, and Scripture is *full* of Sabbath, from start to finish. It even serves to conclude God's creation story. Check out Genesis 2:1-3:

> The heavens and the earth were completed in all
> their vast array.
>
> By the seventh day God had finished the work
> he had been doing; so on the seventh day he rested
> from all his work. Then God blessed the seventh day
> and made it holy, because on it he rested from all the
> work of creating that he had done.

So immediately after creating everything, God . . . rests. Why? Probably because he had worked so hard creating absolutely everything, and he thought to himself, *Dang, I'm wiped out . . . I need a spa day to rejuvenate my muscles!*

But God is the one with what I like to call the

"omnis"—omniscient, omnipresent, and omnipotent—which basically means God can know everything, be everywhere, and do anything. So seriously, why the day of rest?

Think about the order of creation. Land, water, plants, animals . . . and on the sixth day, humans. That means the first thing humans experienced was rest. Why? To remind us—then, now, forever—that we are created beings, that we aren't designed to always be working, *because God is the one who works according to his perfect will and love.*

That seems backward to a lot of us. We run from stillness, in part, because we're trying to earn God's favor. We want to do the work *before* we come to God. We hope to pay God back or give God a good reason to love us. *I know God will start loving me once I stop doing this. I know God will start loving me once I finally . . .*

That's where stillness comes in. We're *meant* to rest. And Sabbath rest can only be found in an intimate relationship with Jesus.

To understand that, though, we need to dig a bit deeper.

Sabbath: Part Two

Let's skip ahead from creation and the first Sabbath all the way to Exodus 20. We're on the slopes of Mount Sinai, and Moses is getting a download from God: a list of ways God's people can be happier and healthier and bring more glory to their Creator. Fourth on that famous list of ten is this:

> Remember the Sabbath day by keeping it holy. Six
> days you shall labor and do all your work, but the

seventh day is a sabbath to the LORD your God. On
it you shall not do any work, neither you, nor your
son or daughter, nor your male or female servant,
nor your animals, nor any foreigner residing in your
towns. For in six days the LORD made the heavens
and the earth, the sea, and all that is in them, but
he rested on the seventh day. Therefore the LORD
blessed the Sabbath day and made it holy.[8]

(I love how God stipulates that not just the person hearing
the commandment needs Sabbath, but everyone else in their
family, business, town, and so on. Why? Because you *know*
some lazy dad would be like, "Look, *I'm* resting today . . . but
you kids? Get out in that field while Daddy puts his feet up!")

Sabbath is an oft-forgotten element of God's instructions for us. We tend to treat it as optional. I love it when
people tell me they're good people and they keep the Ten
Commandments. They usually fall right into my trap.

"Really, you keep the commandments?" I ask.

At that point they have to agree! And they're probably
thinking I'm going to say something about coveting or taking
God's name in vain.

Instead, I ask, "So you keep the Sabbath?"

blank stare and/or questioning grunt

"Yeah," I continue, "every seventh day you take the whole
day off, right? And not just you, but everyone in your family
and everyone who works for you?"

---

[8] Exodus 20:8-11.

I honestly can't remember the last time someone was like, "Yep, I do that!"[9]

But Sabbath is important. It's as Abraham Joshua Heschel said: "Six days a week we wrestle with the world, wringing profit from the earth; on the Sabbath we especially care for the seed of eternity planted in the soul. The world has our hands, but our soul belongs to Someone Else."[10]

I know some of you are thinking something like, *Okay, fine, our need for intimacy is satisfied by stillness. Got it. And Sabbath is God's way of describing stillness. So . . . you're saying we need to take a day off every week, right? Get to the point! TELL ME WHAT TO DO!*

First of all, imaginary reader, I'll get to the point in my own sweet time.

And second, no, I'm not saying that.

I mean, *God* is saying that, for sure. He *already* said it in the Ten Commandments, so that's nothing new.

But what *I'm* saying here is this: You need to satisfy your need for intimacy in the stillness of Jesus. Not by doing more or adding another task to your to-do list. Not by working harder.

Instead, by trusting in Jesus you will enter God's rest.

Jesus Brings an Easy Burden

All right, this is our last section before we end with a few practical ideas. Fair warning: This part is the longest yet. I

---

9 Real quick: Most Christians believe any day of rest can be Sabbath. Church is almost always a part of Sabbath, though some believers—such as pastors, who work on Sundays—take a different day as Sabbath. A minority of Christians believe the Sabbath *must* be on Sunday or Saturday. Either way, Sabbath is both a gift and a command.

10 Abraham Joshua Heschel, *The Sabbath: Its Meaning for Modern Man* (New York: Farrar, Straus and Giroux, 2005), 13.

don't think you'll regret it, though, because it's about Jesus and because it's so full of good news.

Soak in these verses from Hebrews 4:9-10:

> There remains, then, a Sabbath-rest for the people
> of God; for anyone who enters God's rest also rests
> from their works, just as God did from his.

When the Christian church was just getting started, certain groups were trying to make it legalistic. They didn't like the unpredictable nature of God's Spirit, and they didn't like the freedom Jesus had brought. They were saying Christianity was Jesus *plus*: plus rules and regulations and works and family background. And the writer of Hebrews[11] was having none of that.

When Jesus is our Lord, we enter into the rest of Jesus. We step away from our work and rest in his finished work. We step into his Sabbath.

Working more doesn't fill our need for intimacy. And even just "doing" the Sabbath, like checking it off a list, doesn't fill our need either. *Jesus* is the answer to our need for intimacy.

Now even though I'm a pastor, I'm not saying the answer to literally every question is Jesus. If you asked me for a good recipe for chicken parmesan, I wouldn't say, "Jesus." (I would tell you to go ask my grandmother Anita, though!)

But sometimes Jesus is the unexpected answer to un-articulated needs and longings. When we think we're longing

---

[11] We still don't know for sure who wrote Hebrews, by the way.

for relationship, what we really need is intimacy—and the fulfillment of that need is actually not another human, but instead biblical stillness in which we meet Jesus.

Jesus *is* Sabbath. The stillness we're seeking is Jesus himself. When was the last time you entered into the stillness, into the rest, that Jesus bought for you with his perfect life, his death, and his resurrection?

Friends, Jesus brings the rest—the intimate stillness—that our souls are so desperate for.

If you aren't following Jesus, I want to say this to you: I know you're looking for intimacy in other places. We can't live without intimacy. I know because I've tried. I know because I've seen so many other people try. The reality, as St. Augustine wrote to God, is that "our heart is restless until it rests in you."[12]

We will continue to look for intimacy in places that will harm us or in places that cannot truly satisfy us. We will. No matter how much these other things hurt us, no matter how many times we're let down, we keep looking and searching. Our hearts are restless for a reason: God made them that way in order to draw us to himself. When we search for intimacy anywhere besides Jesus, our restlessness increases.

Do you believe there is a place of safety, of relational intimacy, waiting for you?

If you don't, I want to challenge you to choose hope.

If you do, but you haven't found it, hear these words: The answer is Jesus!

---

[12] Saint Augustine, *Confessions*, trans. Henry Chadwick (Oxford: Oxford University Press, 2008), 3.

And if you have found it—if you've felt the truth of Jesus' invitation and promise in Matthew 11:28-30—then you already know that your heart can never be burdened beyond what you can bear:

> Come to me, all you who are weary and burdened, and I will give you rest. Take my yoke upon you and learn from me, for I am gentle and humble in heart, and you will find rest for your souls. For my yoke is easy and my burden is light.

The picture Jesus is using here, which would have been instantly familiar to his listeners, is of a beast of burden, such as an ox or a mule. If you wanted to plow a field in those days or carry a heavy load from A to B, you had two choices: (1) You could try to do the work yourself, or (2) you could place a yoke on your beast and let the beast do the work. That may not be a popular picture these days, but it remains a necessary one. We don't want to think of ourselves as beasts, but the reality is that all of us bear burdens—just like all of us are yoked to something.

Life supplies an endless variety of burdens, doesn't it? It might be your health or your finances. It might be your family or your lack of a family. It might be work or addiction or shame or wealth.

Whatever the burden, we all bear one—and we all know the feeling of being weighed down. Sometimes of being pushed to the ground. Crushed.

Jesus knows this. And when you're still enough, you

know he knows this. Which makes his promise all the more astounding. Know that he will do what he says, no matter how burdened you are.

Jesus is the only one who can promise rest from our burdens, because Jesus is the only one strong enough to take your burden upon himself. He's the only one gracious and loving and merciful enough to want *your* rest more than *his* comfort.

Recently we had this tree in our backyard that needed to come down, so I borrowed an ax from my neighbor and got to work. I was doing the best I could, trying to swing that ax with some awesome velocity, but I'm from New Jersey. The whole outdoors thing is a learning process for me, okay? But I'm trying.[13]

Anyway, before long my son and his two buddies came out to watch and were like, "Cool, can we help?"

So then there was me, all sweaty and trying to put a dent in this tree, and whenever I needed a breather, there was one of these three boys, leaping all around the tree and taking their shirts off and flexing and yelling. It was like a testosterone factory out there.

We were just slamming away at that tree—and I was starting to make some progress, believe it or not—when my wife glanced out the door. She didn't say anything—remember, intimacy doesn't need words!—but she was looking at me like, *What are you doing!*

I asked, "Hey, it's the twenty-first century, babe . . . you want to come help?"

---

[13] And I know I should have used a chain saw. But then we wouldn't have this fun story!

She declined.

We were making such a racket! Chopping, hollering, grunting, you name it. We were *not* going to rest until we got that job done. And before long,[14] the tree finally leaned, cracked, leaned some more, and fell. None too soon, since my arms felt like rubber. And the three boys—all sweaty and sawdusty and panting—were just dancing around the stump, jumping on the fallen tree, crowing about their achievement.

The tree was chopped down. All of us—me and the boys—helped. But I did about 98 percent of the work.

So did the boys really help? Not really.

Did they *feel* like they helped? Absolutely. And they were able to succeed because I took their burden. They were able to rest at the end because they were actually able to *reach* the end.

Friend, when you decide to follow Jesus, this is what happens. He brings the right tools. He does the heavy lifting. He encourages. *He invites you to help and then celebrates you when you do.*

There are people who confront this reality, and their response is: "Man, that's a cop-out. I don't need charity. I don't need someone giving me what I haven't earned."

First of all, I get that. Some of us are prideful almost in a good way. We want to work. We want to pull our own weight.

But second? Stop kidding yourself. *Because none of us can do this.*

It doesn't matter how strong or talented or determined or proud you are . . . you cannot get this done on your own.

---

[14] On a cosmic timescale.

This life, these burdens, this unfulfilled need for intimacy, all of it will crush you.

Jesus isn't your nosy neighbor offering you charity. He isn't shaming you by being nice to you. He's the King of kings and Lord of lords. God in flesh! He's the dude who made hummingbirds and the stars in the farthest-flung galaxy.

Some of us think we *deserve* our burdens. We know Jesus wants to take them, but we want to hold on to them. Then Jesus comes along and takes off our yoke of pride, our yoke of self.

"You actually *can't* do it," he tells us. "You can't do it, but I can, and I've already finished the work."

But we know it's true. And when we let that truth inside ourselves, we realize. We stop white-knuckling life, and we realize.

God's Sabbath is the best possible news because it is the place of greatest intimacy.

In that stillness, we find the wordless intimacy we have always longed for.

And our hearts can rest.

Practice

Keep in mind why we're talking about this stuff. It isn't so we can earn God's favor or love. It's so we can have our need for intimacy met.

Stillness is the way that happens, and as we're painfully aware, stillness is a scarce commodity. It's a discipline, and unless we're intentional about it, we won't experience it.

Be diligent and passionate about seeking intimacy with God. Hebrews 4:11 says, "Let us, therefore, make every effort to enter that rest, so that no one will perish by following their example of disobedience."

It's true of *any* relationship that we need to be diligent and passionate. We need to be dedicated and have a no-quit, never-say-die stubbornness. The more we invest in our relationships with God, the greater the return will be. So keep working at it. We need to make a continual effort. Make a plan, and seek God's grace to continue it . . . and you *will* enter that rest.

We need to divert daily. We need to withdraw weekly. And we need to abandon annually.[15]

One of the barriers to making stillness part of our lives is that we think of stillness as a binary condition. Either we aren't still, or we are. Either we're on social media and watching our shows and chatting at work and listening to music in the car and texting . . . or we live alone in a cave!

That's not the way to make this happen. We need to add more stillness, not to be *only* still.

Every single day you need at least a *little* space. Not everything you do can, or should, involve other people. Divert daily, where it's just you and God. That can be as simple as arriving at work five minutes early and praying in your car. It can even be as simple as driving for five minutes in silence.

You need to recharge weekly. It's a peculiar problem of our culture that we get *exhausted* by our weekends! We've

---

[15] I first encountered this idea on Rick Warren's Twitter (@RickWarren). Rick Warren, Twitter post, August 17, 2009, 4:10 p.m., https://twitter.com/rickwarren/status/3371098693.

taken the idea of Sabbath and flipped it on its head. Instead of a weekly opportunity for rest and intimacy, it's become a weekly opportunity to cram in more: more buying, more traveling, more screen, more selfishness.

And every year you need to abandon your normal context and put yourself in a place where you can be still and know that God is God. If you have a family, take a trip in the car. Camp. Rest. It could be as simple as a day where you take a long hike in silence. The point is to put yourself in a position, at least once a year, to hear from your Father.

Dare to go tech-free.

For an hour, a day, whatever.

Our technology isn't ruining the universe. You can follow Jesus and have a smartphone. You can be led by the Spirit and still check Facebook every day. At the same time, daring yourself to go tech-free for a certain period can have powerful benefits.

My friend Nate, who's a pastor, works on Sundays, so he always takes what he calls "Amish Mondays." He turns his cell off, unplugs the television, and powers down the computer.

Now listen, I love my technology like the next person, but it's a stillness killer. We actually use it to keep away the very stillness we need! So be a rebel and go tech-free.

As we close, remember to seek after the God who speaks in a still, small voice. Intentionally experience God in intimate Sabbath rest. Don't allow yourself to be distracted, and when you are distracted, fight it.

When you find true stillness, you *will* find the true and living God.

1.4

↑ ↙ ↗

learning / deepening

Problem

I want you to do something strange: Look at my picture on the back cover. Then imagine me with no hair.

Terrifying, right?[1]

Contrary to popular belief, however, I didn't spring from the womb covered in all the hair I have now. There *are* hairy babies, for sure, but when I entered the world, there was no hint that I would transform. I looked like a cue ball with arms and legs.

Why do I bring this up?

---

[1] I mentioned in an earlier footnote that I looked like Ryan Gosling, but with dreadlocks. To be honest, that wasn't entirely accurate. I look more like an Italian Bob Marley crossed with a bear . . . who vaguely resembles Ryan Gosling.

Mostly for fun. But I *do* want to talk about babies in general. (My babies, by the way, are definitely the cutest babies ever created—but I digress.) Because whether they're as bald as I was, or whether they're as hairy as the book of Genesis tells us Esau was,[2] all babies have one thing in common: They're the world's best learning machines.

Now there's a whole debate about whether babies are more like blank slates or sponges, whether they're hardwired to learn certain things quickly or whether nature or nurture plays a more pivotal role. But there's one thing everyone agrees on: Babies are crazy good at learning.

In the six short years after we are born, we go from knowing absolutely nothing to being unbelievably gifted creations, unique among any other living creatures on earth. Chimps and dolphins are capable of some amazing things . . . things the average three-year-old can do without breaking a sweat! By the time we reach school age, we're the ones doing science projects and book reports on the rest of the animal kingdom.

Learning doesn't stop in childhood either. When I arrived at Rutgers University in 1994, I found myself in Philosophy 101, and I started *learning*. Like, pontificating-while-sipping-espresso learning. They gave me some Aristotle, a little bit of Nietzsche, a few days with Descartes, and boom, I was like, "Hmm, yes, interesting . . . but have you considered *this*?"

It's funny in hindsight, but it reinforces something. Most of us learn throughout our whole lives as we take up hobbies, become parents, start businesses, and so on. Just as we

---

[2] The NIV says that "his whole body was like a hairy garment" (Genesis 25:25). Another translation (NLT) says he looked as though he were covered in "a fur coat." So, basically, Esau was the first Ewok.

humans are hardwired for relationships, we're also designed to learn. We hunger for knowledge.

Hence our problem.

Remember how often we try to meet our needs the wrong way? Our needs drive our actions. We naturally want to satisfy those needs, so we start looking around—and not everything we try works! Often our needs are only deferred, or temporarily forgotten, rather than met.

And when we do take the time to learn about our actual needs, *all too often it's without coming to a knowledge of God's truth*. This is especially a problem—and a temptation—for our contemporary culture. Most of us have instantaneous access to basically all human knowledge.[3] But so much of the time we're still know-nothing screwups!

God is inviting us to learn, but not for no reason. Rather, God wants our learning to *deepen* us.

Learning is taking in new information.

Deepening is thinking and acting more like Jesus because of new information.

Deepening shapes and changes our hearts and minds and helps us become people of God who are conformed to the image of Jesus.[4]

In this chapter we're looking at the final element in our upward art of living. Remember, as we get our relationship right with God, we learn how to love ourselves in light of that

---

3 I know a family who practice "The Five-Minute Rule," which means you aren't allowed to check any answer online for five minutes. Most of the time you actually *remember* on your own. Other times you forget the question, which means it didn't really matter. And all the time you're less likely to be *that* person who's constantly pulling out a phone in the middle of dinner.

4 I'm about 99 percent sure that I made up the term *deepening*—which I tell you because there's a one percent chance I accidentally stole it. And if I did, and you know from where, give me a call at church and I'll start giving you credit!

relationship, and out of the overflow of God's love and our true identity, we love our neighbors.

Are you ready to learn *and* to deepen? Let's do what we were made to do, and begin to say to God, "I want to learn more—more about how to live, and more about how to be like you."

Promise

God makes us a promise: Our need for learning will be satisfied when we deepen ourselves in God's Word.

Check out Psalm 1:1-3, one of the most beautiful songs ever written about how we relate to God:

> Blessed is the one
>   who does not walk in step with the wicked
> or stand in the way that sinners take
>   or sit in the company of mockers,
> but whose delight is in the law of the LORD,
>   and who meditates on his law day and night.
> That person is like a tree planted by streams of water,
>   which yields its fruit in season
> and whose leaf does not wither—
>   whatever they do prospers.

I want to draw your attention to the word *meditate*. In our culture, we all *sort of* know what that means. Like we clear out our minds or become one with . . . something. And it helps if we're wearing yoga pants and eating kale, right?

In the Word, though, meditation is very different.

Meditate means to chew on something so you can get the nourishment out of it. The Word *feeds* us. It's active and requires us to participate. We've got to think and pray and wrestle and question. That's the word-picture Psalm 1 is giving us. We're being compared to a healthy, flourishing tree beside a stream, and every day we're soaking up all the water and sunlight and nutrients we need to thrive . . . *if* we delight in the Word.

And notice this tree does more than grow: It bears fruit!

That's the deepening we're talking about. Learning that leads us upward, inward, and outward. Learning that brings the Kingdom.

Discernment and Diligence

There's a verse in Paul's second letter to Timothy that captures two important points about deepening in the Word: It takes discernment and diligence.

Paul writes, "Do your best to present yourself to God as one approved, a worker who does not need to be ashamed and who correctly handles the word of truth."[5]

Do you see that phrase "correctly handles"? Things that are beneficial can also be dangerous. Take gasoline. It gets most of us to work in the morning, but you do *not* want to handle it the wrong way. Or water, which is essential for life but can also cause destruction and even death.

That's what Paul is getting at here. The Word is beneficial, but if we don't handle it correctly, we can wield the Word in a way that betrays God's heart.

---

[5] 2 Timothy 2:15.

I'll give you an example. Have you ever listened to a preacher who is angry with everyone? Well, that is *not* handling the Word correctly. God is not angry with you— no matter who you are! The Word tells us that God's anger, which is perfect and righteous anger by the way, was directed at Jesus, who chose to take the bullet for us. There is enough power in the Cross of Jesus to forgive everyone who chooses to follow him. God doesn't love us because we are exceedingly lovable. God loves us because God is love! What does the most famous verse ever say? For God so loved the *world*, right? God loves us so much that he worked out a plan to save us. He sent his Son to live the life we couldn't live, to die the death that we deserve, and to be resurrected from the grave. Which is why Jesus said, "It is finished." The Spirit of God then applies this to our lives, by faith.

When we correctly handle the Word, we are blessed with hope and thankfulness. God isn't mad at us. He loves us like a perfect Father. We can break his heart, but we cannot change his love—just as we cannot change the fact that the perfect work of Jesus is finished and complete, forever.

That's why it's *so* important to be deepened by the Word and not merely to learn facts about it. Our learning needs to grow us, changing the way we think and act. Changing us to be more like Jesus.

We're sinful people, all of us. And the irony is that we can get the Word right but God's *heart* wrong . . . which means we're actually getting the Word wrong!

So discernment is vital, but so is diligence. Here's our verse again, with the next important phrase highlighted:

"*Do your best* to present yourself to God as one approved, a worker who does not need to be ashamed and who correctly handles the word of truth."

Other translations add the nuance of being diligent and working hard. Even more, of having persistent zeal. Being deepened by the Word—something that transforms us into workers approved by God—takes serious effort. And that doesn't match our culture's messaging . . . even our Christian culture!

We've got Bible apps and websites. We've got tons of useful and unique translations. We have books and podcasts and worship music and church options and online curriculums and Christian schools.

Those things are good.

But none of them is a substitute for spending our own time in the Word.

One of the truths Jesus used to defeat Satan's temptation was that we "shall not live on bread alone, but on every word that comes from the mouth of God."[6]

Just as we need to work in order to provide physical food for ourselves and our families, we also need to work to nourish ourselves with the Word. We need to be eager and even zealous to do that.

It's like when we make a resolution to lose some of those holiday pounds. Most of us diet for about three days and go to the gym once, and then . . . we stop. (Okay, maybe that's just me—but now there's more of me to love!) Unsurprisingly, the resolution remains a dream. But it's not an *impossible*

---

[6] Matthew 4:4.

dream. There *are* people who resolve to lose weight or get in shape, and they pull it off! What those people have in common is persistence. If they keep showing up at the gym, even when they don't feel like it, they'll get results. If they keep eating oatmeal instead of donuts for breakfast, they'll get results.

Deepening in the Word is the same. We need to keep showing up. We need to keep fighting for it—because we *know* Satan is fighting *against* us. Have you ever noticed that you can sit down and open your Bible, and all of a sudden the phone rings off the hook? Or the kids have a meltdown, or the freezer starts making a weird clunking noise? Pretty soon you forget about deepening—all you want to do is watch YouTube until you fall asleep!

Satan can't stand it when we immerse ourselves in the Word, because God uses the Word to change our hearts and to make us more like Jesus.

And Satan *hates* that.

So you need to be a straight-up rebel. Push back at Satan. Read extra. Plug your ears and keep reading. Do your *best*, not your "almost best."

Second Timothy 3:17 says that through the Word "the servant of God may be thoroughly equipped for every good work." That means if you're being deepened by the Word, you'll be overqualified for every good work God has designed for you!

Memorization and the Nature of the Word

One of the best ways to handle the Word correctly is to memorize it.

King David talked about hiding God's Word in his heart,

about waking up in the middle of the night and having his first thought be about the Word.

Now that doesn't need to be a dramatic undertaking. There's this guy who has all of John's Gospel memorized, and he does a one-man show with it. I'm not saying we need to memorize an entire book, starting tomorrow.

Me, I'm more of a one-verse guy. I'll write out a verse on an index card and keep that in my pocket until I learn it. I'll reach for my wallet while I'm waiting at Starbucks, and I'll pull out my card.

Or you can put a verse on the lock screen of your phone. Tape it to the dashboard in your car or to the mirror in the bathroom where you brush your teeth. Set your computer to notify you once a day with a verse until you've got it memorized. And no matter how bad you think you are at memorizing, you're actually good at it! Seriously, if you're reading this book, you are more than capable of memorizing tons of verses.

How do we know this is actually a useful or necessary idea, though?

One reason is simple observation: The believers throughout history who have been the most like Jesus, and made the biggest difference in the Kingdom, have been absolutely soaked in the Word.[7]

An even better reason is the nature of the Bible. We use the Word as our reference point because all our *other* reference points are a lot less stable!

Here's an easy example: parenting. Every generation learns

---

[7] I don't have space to show this here. But if you doubt me, choose any amazing Christian and check out his or her biography. If that person was sorta like, "Meh . . ." about Scripture, I'll buy you a bacon cheeseburger with extra jalapenos!

updated information about baby safety, and then there's a conflict between the new parents and the grandparents, right? As my grandma Anita would say, "If baby's teething, just rub a little bourbon on her gums." And my sister would say, "Grandma! You can't give alcohol to a baby—they have medicine for that now!"[8]

Or think about auto safety. My folks grew up before seat belts were standard in cars. Nowadays, we have seat belts *and* airbags. The next generation will probably cruise around in driverless cars that are completely crashproof.

The point is that every culture gets some things right and some things wrong. The Word, however, is the same yesterday, today, and forever.

(This is one part of one chapter, not a whole book, so of course there are nuances we can't get into here. Culture absolutely influences how we understand the Word, sometimes in ways we aren't even aware of. Having said that, however, the Word is *still* the way to get outside the limitations of our culture, our upbringing, our past, and so on.)

See, God's Word is transgenerational. It's transcultural and transnational and transpolitical. It shows us things like self-sacrificial love, mercy, forgiveness, and grace that are *never* stylish. Those are eternal truths, not cultural norms. When we're being deepened by the Word, we're being shown an entirely different way to live. It's through the Word that we see life, like a pair of glasses that helps us see everything else clearly. Read Hebrews 4:12:

---

[8] Of course my sister turned out fine after Grandma rubbed bourbon on *her* gums!

The word of God is alive and active. Sharper than
any double-edged sword, it penetrates even to
dividing soul and spirit, joints and marrow; it judges
the thoughts and attitudes of the heart.

That means the Word can divide what is indivisible. God can divide our thoughts, intentions, feelings, motivations. The Word is like a nanoscalpel that cuts directly to what truly matters. Whatever we struggle with, God's Word fights back. If we struggle with fear or shame or pride or lust or gluttony, the Word fights back with unstoppable power!

And that's why we hide the Word in our hearts—because when it's in our hearts, it comes out in our lives. When we are deepened by the Word, it satisfies our need for learning. We are always learning new things because God is always teaching us how to think and act more like Jesus.

This is a huge deal.

Culture is telling us to hate our enemies, and God is helping us learn how to love our enemies. Culture is telling us not to bother loving someone unless they're lovable, and God is helping us learn how to love everyone.

Look, this might be a strange thing for an author and pastor to say, but if the only time you study the Word is at church or in books like this, *you're never going to become who God has created you to be.*

The Word Calls Us on Our Stuff

We've seen how we need discernment and diligence to be deepened by the Word. And how Satan fights against that, because the nature of the Word is to make us more like Jesus. But . . . this doesn't sound *that* hard. If the Word is so important, why do so many Christians fail to spend time in it?

That's a good question with an uncomfortable answer. Here's what Paul says about it in 2 Timothy 3:14-17:

> As for you, continue in what you have learned and have become convinced of, because you know those from whom you learned it, and how from infancy you have known the Holy Scriptures, which are able to make you wise for salvation through faith in Christ Jesus. All Scripture is God-breathed and is useful for teaching, rebuking, correcting and training in righteousness, so that the servant of God may be thoroughly equipped for every good work.

Okay, ready?

We don't spend as much time in the Word as we want to, or need to, because when we read the Word, we *will* be corrected.

The Spirit of God, entering our hearts and minds when we read the Word, is one of the main ways God calls us out on our stuff.

And we don't always want to be corrected, right?

I'm being as real as I can here. Sometimes we have this heavy feeling about the Word, almost like we don't have the energy to work on something else in our lives—or even because we *want* to keep doing something we know we shouldn't.

Sometimes it's big. Have you ever heard (or said), "I could

never forgive them for what they did!" Then we read Jesus telling us, "If you do not forgive others their sins, your Father will not forgive your sins."[9]

Sometimes it's small. I can get my "Italian frustration face" on, and everything that comes at me makes me grumble. Then I read, "Do all things without grumbling"[10] and I'm like, "*Come on*, Lord, I really need to grumble right now!"

Our culture tells us that if someone corrects us, that person don't love us. We're told that love means everyone is free to do whatever they want whenever they want.

Wrong.

Love corrects. That isn't *all* love does, but it is absolutely part of what love does.

Picture a parent. A parent who never corrects and directs a child does not love that child, because that child will run into traffic and eat cleaning products and detonate fireworks in his hands. We're all people in progress. We don't just need correction . . . we should *want* correction. We should want to be more loving, more forgiving, wiser, more generous.

But usually we don't.

Which is why it's vital to be in the Word, habitually and diligently, so God's Spirit can get to work on us. Day in, day out.

The Word is God's way of mirroring back to us what life in the Spirit looks like, and what *we* look like. And unless you're already perfect, you don't look as much like Jesus as you could.

Hebrews 4:13 says, "Nothing in all creation is hidden

---

9 Matthew 6:15.
10 Philippians 2:14, ESV.

from God's sight. Everything is uncovered and laid bare before the eyes of him to whom we must give account."

We live in a world of scandals, so it's terrifying to think of everything uncovered and laid bare. Are you doing something no one knows about? Not even your spouse or boss or parents or kids?

God knows.

But remember what it says in 2 Timothy 2:15: that we can present ourselves to God *and not be ashamed*!

Deepening is the way we can stand before God, with our whole life opened, and see him smile.

See, we don't get to choose the terms of our existence. We "live and move and have our being" in Christ.[11] That's the way it is. Our lives have been gifted to us by the true and living God. The same God, by the way, who loved us before we were born, knit us together in the womb, and prepared amazing Kingdom works for us to accomplish.

Maybe it's time we gave our Creator the benefit of the doubt and tried living the way he designed us.

Maybe it's time for us to open the Word and dive in and go deep.

Practice

⬆ *Ways of reading:* One of the things that I've learned as a student of the Word is that sometimes you take a plane, sometimes you take a car, and sometimes you walk. What's important is that you're traveling.

---

[11] Acts 17:28.

⬆ Overview: We can fly from coast to coast in about five or
six hours, and if the weather's good, we can learn a lot
about this country. We can see mountain ranges, cities,
deserts, and prairies. We get a sense of where things are
and how they connect.

That's the thirty-thousand-foot view of the Bible. To get that,
read the whole book in a year. If you've never done it, you
should. And honestly? It's not complicated and only takes
about as long each day as watching the nightly news. There
are a kajillion plans out there, but basically you read three
chapters of the Old Testament and one chapter of the New
Testament each day.

⬆ Engaging: Sometimes we'd rather drive than fly. We can
slow down in our cars. We can stop when we want to. We
get a street-level view of neighborhoods and people. We
can take detours.

That's another way to view the Bible. To get it, read a chapter. Read another one the next day. Go through the same
book of the Bible for a month, reading only a chunk or two
each day. Get to know the overall point of John, Exodus, or
Colossians.

⬆ Meditating: Other times it's all about a slow stroll. When we
walk, we can literally stop and smell the flowers. We can
crouch down or look up. We understand things with more of
our senses than mere sight.

This is about soaking in a few sentences or even a few words. Like cloth in dye, we want to take on all the colors of a specific passage. A great way to read the Bible is to go slowly and intentionally, seeking to extract all the nourishment out of a verse or few words.

⬆ *Scheduling:* We make time every day for what is important to us. We make sure our schedules allow us to shower and eat. We even make time for our favorite TV shows and our hobbies.

Following God is not a hobby. We should strive to be in the Word every day. Make the time. Figure it out. Change your schedule. You *can* do it too! Try getting to work five minutes early and reading in your car. Have your smartphone app read the Word to you while you run on the treadmill. And for those of you with busy home lives, don't forget to get a "Potty Bible" and linger a little longer in the bathroom! The point is to be creative *and* persistent. Find something that works.

⬆ *Journaling:* One of my favorite things is to journal along with what I'm reading in the Word. I write out questions and ideas and hopes. It's important to write down the things that God is speaking to me, specifically and uniquely as I read his living Word, and journaling is also a great way to "get clear" on stuff I'm struggling with.

⬆ *Points to Ponder:* Take an inventory of your relationship with God's Word. Are you satisfied with how much time you spend reading the Word? How does your life change when you are immersed in the Word? What is your plan for being deepened by God's Word?

OUR CULTURE TELLS US, "You need to learn to love yourself!"

God tells us, "You need to learn to love yourself!"

Wait . . . what?

Here's the deal: Those identical statements mean nearly opposite things. Our culture wants us to love ourselves by putting ourselves first.[1] This is incredibly destructive. It's the reason relationships rip apart, because you have two people putting themselves first, instead of the other person. It's why Paul told Timothy, "There will be terrible times in the last days. People will be lovers of themselves."[2] It's the reason our public discourse is poisonous and the reason Americans spend more than a billion dollars each year on teeth whiteners.[3]

Good thing Jesus was sent on a rescue mission.

See, what God means by loving ourselves is incredibly powerful. We love and value ourselves based on the finished work of the cross of Jesus. At the Cross, our identity is displayed in God's grace and love.

Don't miss this: The only way to love ourselves in the way that God desires is to see ourselves through the lens of the cross of Jesus. Jesus spirituality is all about *Jesus*. And everyone knows that the cross and the empty tomb is what Jesus is all about.

But when was the last time you thought, *Loving myself has everything to do with the cross and empty tomb of Jesus?*

Exactly.

The death and resurrection of Jesus, and our trust in him,

[1] There's a simple reason, by the way: so we'll be less content and spend more money on ourselves!
[2] 2 Timothy 3:1-2.
[3] "Teeth Whitening: How to Whiten Teeth—Teeth Bleaching," *What's Cooking America*, https:// whatscookingamerica.net/HealthBeauty/TeethWhitening.htm.

places us in the family of God. In order to properly love ourselves, we need a clear vision of who we are. God's perfect plan was for us to view ourselves through the lens of the cross. God wants us to view ourselves as he views us, in and through Jesus.

We just don't think about it that way. But we need to. We were re-created in Christ to think about ourselves this way. And when we understand our truest identity, the one given to us by God in Christ, then truly biblical self-love ensues.

The last part of the greatest commandment—"love your neighbor as yourself"—is impossible *unless* we love ourselves. That's what *as* means—"in the same way." We need to love our neighbors in the same way that we love ourselves.

Which is to say, we're *commanded* to love ourselves, but we've got to do it God's way.

Remember, our needs and longings are given to us by our Creator, and they point us back to the only one who can satisfy them. Each one of us has a very deep need of self-love. And we chose to satisfy that need in different ways. But unless we see ourselves in Christ, we will learn the words of that great English theologian Mick Jagger: "I can't get no satisfaction."

As we focus on the Cross of Jesus, we will examine our need for honesty, self-control, intentionality, and humility. Because only by seeing ourselves as Jesus sees us, and living and loving out of that place, can we truly satisfy those deep needs.

Are you ready to look in?

honesty / reflection

Problem

We love to tell people, "Be honest with me."

But do we really want the answers to that statement?

It's like when Lynn and I were newly married, maybe two weeks in, and we were about to go out and meet some friends. Lynn came out of the bedroom and asked the question that husbands have dreaded since the Garden of Eden. As the words came toward me, I felt like I was watching a train wreck in slow motion.

"Does this look good on me?"

I was flabbergasted. I mean, I knew this day would come. But so soon? And right before we went out? No good could come from this. This was a surefire way to absolutely annihilate the fragile "honeymoon" period of our new family. I was truly scared and—so unlike me—absolutely speechless.

Suddenly Lynn flashed one of her radiant smiles. That freaked me out even more. I started to plan out my own obituary: *Young pastor's wife loses her mind on her husband, and he drops dead from fear* . . .

"Oh, Daniel. Don't worry. I really want to know. My dad was always really honest with me about those things, and I'd like for you to be also."

Now my momma didn't raise no dummy. This was my first real "husband test." And it was a nasty one. I'd heard what she'd asked, but what was she actually saying? I realized I was upstream with no paddle.

"Daniel, I really mean it. Just tell me what you think. I really want to know."

So I took a deep breath, tried to get some saliva in my parched mouth, and wiped the sweat off my brow.

"Sweetheart, you look beautiful." And I waited for what seemed like an eternity.

She smiled and said, "Really?"

"Really."

"Thanks. But I really don't like it, so I'm going to change. But thanks for your honesty. I really appreciate it."

And she turned and went back to the closet. I stood shell-shocked—what on earth just happened?

I tell this story because often we're willing to ask for what we don't need, which is fake honesty from others, but we're reluctant to ask for what we truly need, which is real honesty from ourselves.

Even though we know we need it.

Crucially, this need for honesty involves our entire being. We need to be honest about everything that makes us *us*. And at the deepest, most fundamental level, this means spiritual honesty, which involves who we are in light of who God is.

Without honesty, we aren't living in reality. Without honesty, at best, we're simply playacting, and at worst, we're completely deceived. We desperately need honesty—and that need for honesty, God promises, is satisfied when we practice the art of reflection.

We'll spend the rest of the chapter looking at what reflection is. Real quick, though, let's define what honesty means. There's absolutely no deep, hidden meaning in the etymology of the word. I'm not going to blow your minds here: Honesty is being truthful, fair, and sincere. It's having integrity. It's being upfront about who we are at all levels, inside and out.

I think we all know what honesty is, mostly because we feel it when we're *not* being honest.

But we also all know that being truly honest is really, *really* hard.

Promise

Let's turn to our Scripture passage for this chapter. It comes from Matthew's Gospel, and the whole thing is Jesus speaking to his disciples. (By the way, when you see the term "Son of Man," that's one of the ways Jesus refers to himself.)

> Jesus said to his disciples, "Whoever wants to be
> my disciple must deny themselves and take up their

cross and follow me. For whoever wants to save their life will lose it, but whoever loses their life for me will find it. What good will it be for someone to gain the whole world, yet forfeit their soul? Or what can anyone give in exchange for their soul? For the Son of Man is going to come in his Father's glory with his angels, and then he will reward each person according to what they have done."[1]

We're going to use these verses to shine a light on three aspects of honesty. First, what we're really like as people. Second, what Jesus is really like. And third, why it's so important to be honest about our motivations.

I'm going to be especially honest in this chapter—which kind of makes sense, right?—so get ready!

Be Honest about Our Sin

Okay, let's talk reflection. Because if we're going to meet our need for honesty, we've got to get an accurate picture of what we look like.

Simply put, reflection is self-honesty before Jesus. Better than our reflection in a mirror, reflection in the face of Jesus shows us our truest selves, inside and out. Not just what others see about us, and not what we can comfortably admit. Our true selves aren't even what our best friends know about us. All of those are, to an extent, false reflections.

Let me show you what I mean with an actual conversation—which seems like a fake conversation, I realize!

---

[1] Matthew 16:24-27.

Dude: Man, I'm totally a good person!

Me: How do you know?

Dude: Well, it's not like I'm Charles *Manson*!

Me: Stop it! You're not a good person just because you're *not* on death row for murder!

Dude: What am I, *Hitler*?

Me: Just because you're not the *worst* possible version of yourself doesn't actually mean you're good!

Look, if we're going to check out our reflection in a mirror and be truthful about who we are, let's make sure it's a real mirror.

Our need for honesty will only be satisfied when we compare ourselves to Jesus. And here's why: Jesus was the perfect human, without sin, while absolutely all of us *do* sin. That difference is what allows the comparison. Jesus is the only objective, unchanging standard for what it means to be human.

Now you might be one of those people who's like, "Bro, why all this focus on sin? You pastors are always on about sin, sin, sin. Can't you be positive for five seconds? There's good in everyone!"

I don't disagree with you in a sense. We *do* talk about sin all the time. (So did Jesus, by the way!) And people *can* do some amazingly good things.

Here's the deal, though: There's a right and a wrong way to talk about sin. You can talk about sin in every chapter of a book, every sermon, every conversation, *and still be hopeful and encouraging*.

So I am going to talk about sin—a lot—but I'm going to show you why being honest about our sin is wonderful news.

And before we go any further, here's the definition of sin I'm going to be using: Sin is the simple reality that no human, except for Jesus, has ever been as good as they could have been.

It's that stark. Have all your actions and thoughts and motivations *always* been the best possible? Are you, and have you always been, perfect? If not, you're a sinner.

Sin is not being bad some of the time or all the time—it's failing to be as good as we could be.

Here's an example. My wife and I have been married for twelve years now. And recently I finally *got* it: What my wife really wants and needs from me is love. In some ways, every husband wants to be Mr. Fix-It. When something breaks, we fix it. For my first eleven-plus years of marriage that is exactly what happened—I would immediately grab my screwdriver and toss on my bandanna and be like, "Babe, I'm gonna fix this for you!"

But this time my brain and heart and hands finally got the message. So when my wife told me about the problem, the first thing I did was give her a big hug and say, "Sweetie, I love you so much, and I'm so grateful for you."

She was impressed. It only took me a smidge over a decade! She was like, "You're doing so good right now."[2]

It might seem weird for me to say this, but in this specific area *I'd been sinning ever since I got married.* I hadn't been doing anything wrong, exactly—but I hadn't been doing things as *right* as I could have. I'd been lacking some of the fruit of the Spirit in that area, such as love, kindness, and gentleness.

---

[2] And *then* I tied my bandanna on and fixed it.

What's interesting—and very biblical—is that our best moments of growth and learning often reveal how badly we've been missing the mark up to that point.

The reason is that we see Jesus, and then we see us, and all of a sudden the light bulb goes on.

We realize that Jesus is the one person who can say, "Yes, I pleased God, not only in action but also in motivation—100 percent of the time."

Us . . . not so much.

That's hard to hear, because we want to be good people. But it's honest.

Be Honest about Whom You Follow

Our need for honesty is satisfied by reflection as we humbly compare ourselves to Jesus.

Except why should we compare ourselves to Jesus in the first place? Who said that was the standard?

Well, Jesus did!

And many of us reading this book will claim to follow Jesus. The tricky thing is that lots of people *say* they're following Jesus but don't actually compare their lives honestly to the example of Jesus.

The reason for that is understandable. We have a lot of stuff going on in our lives. Families, jobs, church, savings accounts, vacations, car trouble, diets, report cards . . . the list goes on for what feels like forever. So we look at all that, and we want to do well. We want to handle things the right way. We even ask ourselves, "What would Jesus do?"

Oops.

Time to check our reflection with Jesus again.

Jesus had an insanely hectic life, just like we do. And we know the answer to the question, "What would Jesus do?" *He made his relationship with the Father the absolute priority.*

Jesus put God first. That's what we need to do. No matter how well we think we can handle something—our finances, our kids, our work—we need to make Jesus our priority. We need to make Jesus our foundation and our standard before we do anything else.

What would Jesus do: invest in a Roth IRA or in real estate? The real answer is that he'd *pray*. A ton. He'd get up early and make time to stand before God, honestly and openly. He'd make that the priority before he even thought of doing anything else.

The Bible has a great example of our human temptation to follow Jesus *once* . . . and then rely on our own goodness and skill and hard work. The apostle Paul was your classic overachiever. No matter what his job was—initially hunting down Christians so he could imprison and kill them, or later introducing people to Jesus—he gave it everything he had.

(He was also one of the original humblebraggers, by the way. In Philippians 3:3-6, he wrote that he puts "no confidence in the flesh," but then admits he has really good reasons for such confidence . . . and then he goes on to list six or seven reasons why he's awesome.)

So here's Paul, coming to the city of Corinth. He wants to make sure the Corinthian believers follow Jesus the right way. And Corinth isn't some town in the sticks. It's an important city with a seven-hundred-year history. The people there are going to respect and value Paul's qualifications.

But Paul does the right thing. He looks at his reflection, compared to Jesus.

And he brings with him exactly one qualification: that he knows and follows the crucified and risen Lord.[3]

For us to be truly honest and to truly know ourselves, the one we follow needs to be everything.

In fact, when Paul writes to the believers in Galatia, he says something along the same lines: that he's determined not to boast or brag about *anything* . . . except the Cross of Jesus.

Basically he's saying, "I'm following the King of kings, relentlessly, and *nothing* is going to get in the way of that."

This is why Jesus needs to be at the center. Of everything. If we need to understand something fundamental about ourselves, about God, about the world . . . *all* of that starts with Jesus, at the Cross.

Which takes us right back to our main scripture: "Whoever wants to be my disciple must deny themselves and take up their cross and follow me."[4]

We all know the cross was a method of execution. If you were condemned to death on a cross, you were required to carry part of your cross to the execution site.

That's the imagery Jesus is working with. And it leads to one of the most difficult—and honest—sentences in this book: *Death to self isn't merely a prerequisite of following Jesus but a continuing characteristic.*

---

3 Check out 1 Corinthians 2.
4 Matthew 16:24.

We sometimes think—or we're told by our culture—that the notion of "death to self" or even self-denial is the worst possible way to live. It's barbaric and backward. We're meant to live, and we're meant to do that by self-actualizing and self-improving and self-directing.

The confusion arises because we equate self-denial with a lack of self-esteem. But the opposite is true: Followers of Jesus should have the absolute *highest* self-esteem possible *because* of their self-denial.

In life there's a constant choice. God's Word often contrasts it as a choice between the Spirit and the flesh—by which it means the things of God and the things we naturally revert to as humans. That's why following Jesus *continually* is such a challenge for us, because God is asking his children to set aside our natural priorities, like selfishness and pride and jealousy, and instead take up his list of priorities. Love, joy, and peace. Patience even when the situation is incredibly stressful or aggravating. Kindness and goodness, especially to those who we think don't deserve it. Faithfulness in response to infidelity. A spirit so filled with grace that it can risk being gentle. Self-control.

When we reflect honestly on ourselves—and on the nature of Jesus—the bad news becomes good news.

We have no idea how to live by God's priorities, but *God* knows how we can do that. In fact, God did more than design us to live his way . . . God also *empowers* us by his Spirit to live his way. It's like God gives us a road map *and* the vehicle that will take us there.

So we can say to God, "Lord, I have no idea how to love

that person, so will you show me? I want to follow your priorities and your wisdom."

That's exactly what Jesus meant when he told us to deny ourselves, take up our crosses, and follow him.

And when we do that, we discover a level of personal joy and satisfaction that astounds the world.

Look, it's not wrong to want to be the good ones—as long as our goodness comes from Christ! That goodness fills us when we are honest about our own lack of perfect goodness. We don't get the medicine we need from our doctors unless we're honest, right? Once we admit we're sick, we can be healed.

I've got to be honest about the sin in my own heart. As a father, am I the most patient? No. Am I the most affirming and encouraging? No. As a husband, am I the best friend I could be? No. As a pastor, am I the most faithful in prayer? No. In service? No.

The beauty is that these failures don't define how bad or messed up I am. Rather, they show that God is present and working in my life, because these are areas in which God's Spirit can continue to transform me. To make *me* look more like Jesus.

Here's what King David—whom the Bible calls "a man after God's own heart"[5]—says in Psalm 51:1-4:

Have mercy on me, O God,
   according to your unfailing love;
according to your great compassion
   blot out my transgressions.

---

5 Acts 13:22.

Wash away all my iniquity
    and cleanse me from my sin.

For I know my transgressions,
    and my sin is always before me.
Against you, you only, have I sinned
    and done what is evil in your
        sight;
so you are right in your verdict
    and justified when you judge.

He says he has sinned against only God. And this is after committing adultery, treason, and murder.

So at the very least he's sinned against a husband, his nation, and a fellow human.

Which is why it's so interesting he confesses that his sin is against *only* God. David is so concerned with reflection—with knowing his true self—that he speaks only about how his actions have hurt God. (And where do you think God's Spirit would move David next? Exactly: to also reflect and repent of the ways his sin has hurt *others*.)

If we follow Jesus, we follow someone who was tempted in *every* way, like us, yet who was perfect. And who *is* eternal.

We cannot look at ourselves in any reflection other than the face of Jesus.

When we are tempted, we often stumble—but not Jesus! He shows what real living is all about. And when we see ourselves reflected in the perfection of Jesus, our failings take on great clarity.

Yet we take heart, for this is the same Jesus who looks at our sin with love and calls us to a better way.

Be Honest about Why You Follow

We need to be honest about ourselves.

And we need to be honest about who it is we follow.

Without those two truths, we can't understand *why* to follow Jesus in the first place. Let's hit our scripture one more time, because Jesus knew his followers would need a clear reason for choosing what is, admittedly, the more difficult way to live:

> Jesus said to his disciples, "Whoever wants to be my disciple must deny themselves and take up their cross and follow me. For whoever wants to save their life will lose it, but whoever loses their life for me will find it. What good will it be for someone to gain the whole world, yet forfeit their soul? Or what can anyone give in exchange for their soul? For the Son of Man is going to come in his Father's glory with his angels, and then he will reward each person according to what they have done.[6]

Now obviously following Jesus doesn't instantly kill most of us.[7] So what does losing our lives mean?

Think of it with basic economic principles. It works like this: I'll pay you something, and you provide me something.

---

6 Matthew 16:24-27.
7 Though people are killed every day around the world for following Jesus.

From that come a million permutations, because we have different things we want and different amounts we're willing to pay, right? Like for some people, buying six pounds of coffee for fifty dollars is a good deal, but other people are willing to pay two hundred and fifty dollars for the same amount!

At the end of the day, a satisfied consumer is someone who says, "I value the product or service I received more than I value the cash I parted with."

That's what Jesus is getting at in this verse about losing—and finding—our lives.

We all follow this principle.

The athlete gives up things now—donuts, lounging on the couch—to gain something later. The parent gives up things now—sleep, money—to gain something later. The young teacher gives up things now—switching schools, freedom to choose which classes to teach—to gain tenure.

Jesus is taking something we all understand and applying it to the eternal. And what he is saying *only* makes sense if we exist after death.

What's the point of having absolutely *everything* for a single day, he's asking, if you're going to *lose* everything for the rest of your life? And because of eternity, it's even *more* radical.

God's Word tells us that after we die we will continue to exist, meet God, and be judged by God—and live forever in resurrected bodies.

Now we could debate some of these particulars, but we won't, since we want to keep the focus on the main thing. See, if we exist forever, then even if we live to be one hundred, *this life is less than a fraction of a fraction of a fraction of eternity.*

Which leads to one of my favorite parts about God. It's a creative move only God could dream up, let alone pull off. Watch this.

- If we live for ourselves in this life, *nothing* we do in this life will last into eternity.

- If we live for God in this life, *every good thing* we do in this life will also become infinitely better in eternity.

Isn't that amazing? Like if I love my kids, I get to enjoy loving my kids now—and in eternity. If I introduce someone to Jesus, I get to enjoy that now—and in eternity.

If we're living for ourselves, we're virtually the walking dead. We may look normal to most people, but the truth is we're a zombie apocalypse.

And this idea of motivation—of choosing God's way now because of eternity—is completely countercultural. Our culture is all about the now. Faster, quicker, easier. For example, how did we even survive before streaming media and two-day shipping?

The unintended result of all that convenience is that we have trouble thinking long-term. We fail to think consequentially. But the plans and purposes of God, unlike ours, *never hinge on expediency*. God's plans hinge on God's perfect will. If God wills something, God accomplishes that thing . . . regardless of how long it takes or how easy it is.

And here's God's master plan: God wants to be glorified; God desires that no one should perish; God wants the whole world to function in perfect harmony and oneness (shalom).

God's plan for accomplishing this? People! I mean, without even breaking a sweat we could come up with a million ways to improve that plan, right? Using people to accomplish God's plan seems like a *terrible* idea! We stink at so many of the things God values . . . and a lot of what we're good at goes against the heart of God.

It's like God were the general manager of an NFL team, and on draft day he looked up at the board and said, "Forget all these guys. Who's the absolute *worst* college player? Who's the practice-squad guy from the college team ranked dead last? Okay . . . I'll take that guy with my first pick. I'm going to build my team around him."

We don't like to think of ourselves like that, but guess what? We're even lamer than that guy. We're like that guy's little brother's nerdy friend who can't even walk across the room without tripping.

God's always been doing it this way.

When God picked the Israelites, they weren't *from* a weak nation . . . Israel *wasn't* a nation, period.

Don't get me started on the disciples. Bumbling, selfish, clueless.

And Paul. He's the guy who was trying to murder God's team members, literally, and God puts him in charge of the earliest churches.

I could name dozens of other examples from Scripture and thousands of examples from history. Every single one has something in common: willingness.

That's what God's looking for. When you're honest with yourself about who you really are, your list of qualifications blows up in your face. You've got *nothing* to offer. Expect your willingness. Except yourself.

So let's be willing to offer ourselves—our honest-to-God, sinful selves. Let's follow the only one who gives us a perfect reflection. And let's do it with the knowledge that God's future is forever.

Actions Reveal

I want to close this chapter with one quick thought: *What we do shows who we are.*

Listen to Jesus in Matthew 15:16-20:

> "Are you still so dull?" Jesus asked them. "Don't you see that whatever enters the mouth goes into the stomach and then out of the body? But the things that come out of a person's mouth come from the heart, and these defile them. For out of the heart come evil thoughts—murder, adultery, sexual immorality, theft, false testimony, slander. These are what defile a person; but eating with unwashed hands does not defile them."

It's that simple—and that hard. James talks about the same thing, over and over. So do the Old Testament prophets.

Sometimes Christians will freak out here. *You're saying we're saved by works, by what we do . . . you're saying we* earn *our salvation!*

Nope. Works are evidence. What we do—actions, words, even thoughts—show the condition of our heart.

Remember our key passage for this chapter, where we learn that Jesus "is going to come in his Father's glory with his angels, and then he will reward each person according to what they have done"?

The books are going to be open. Our online lives are going to be printed out. Each relationship and job and hobby and credit card statement and phone call will be spread out on the table.

I can sum that up in two words: *Actions reveal.*

And I can sum up our reaction—okay, fine, *my* reaction—in two words as well: *Holy. Moly.*[8]

That's terrifying, isn't it?

Except God is not done with us yet.

Hear that again.

God is not done with us yet.

Friends, this is why we follow Jesus. This is why we invite his Spirit into our lives. This is why we give glory to the Father.

None of us is perfect or can be perfect. *All* of us will stand before God, with eternity open before us.

This is the best of all outcomes.

Because when we know who we really are, and who we're really following, and why, *God's judgment holds no terror*. God is working in us, growing us, changing us, and loving us without limit. If we follow him, we can't be afraid to come

---

8 Or insert your favorite, totally appropriate word here. I was thinking *cannoli* but realized that many people have never experienced the bliss of a cannoli from New York.

before him because we *know* we're safe in his love, all because of Jesus.

Let me speak some truth to you. And I mean *you*, the individual reading this right now. I may not know you personally, but I know the following is true: God isn't surprised about or scared of you right now because he already knows you and loves you. God will never leave you or forsake you. Anything—*anything*—you're suffering isn't worthy of comparison with the eternal joy set before you.

That's why we can be honest. That's why we can practice reflection. No matter how bad your batting average is as a Christian, it's never too late. If you've struck out over and over, and you can't even foul off a single pitch, come to God right now and say, "Jesus, do a work in me. I want to follow you. I want honesty, and I need grace."

Let me tell you, if you say that to God, with all your heart, you're going to hit it out of the park, and Jesus is going to be high-fiving you as you come around third, okay?

When we see ourselves reflected in Jesus, honestly, we're exactly where God wants us.

Completely vulnerable.

Filled to the brim with hope.

Practice

⚓ Be honest with yourself.

⚓ Our need for honesty is satisfied when we speak the truth about who we are and who Jesus is. Consider speaking the truth about yourself. This can happen in a journal or even in your car on the way to work. Dare to name yourself and what you do out loud—and know that God is listening with love.

✅ Be honest about whom you follow.

✅ The best way to know Jesus is to read Scripture and pray. Challenge yourself to read one of the Gospels—or all of them! Keep a journal handy, and write down anything that is surprising, encouraging, challenging, troubling, healing, and so on. Then pray about it!

✅ Be honest about *why* you follow Jesus.

✅ The Christian life is definitely not the easiest life—but it's the most satisfying and joyful life. Make a list of things you have to give up to follow Jesus. Then make a list of things you will gain by following Jesus.

✅ Be aware that actions reveal.

✅ Think about everything you do during a typical week. Work, play, family, church, community, relaxing, and so on. Be as specific as you'd like. When you're done, think about what the list says about your heart. What did you do *more* of than you expected? Are the things you claim to be important reflected in the way you spend your time and money?

2.2

↑ ↙ ↗

self-control / fasting

Problem

If you have kids, I'm sure you'll agree that there's always one crystal-clear memory from around the time they were born. I want to share something that happened just before my second child, Maranatha, was born.

The story starts with my wife, who is one of those women who is *not* going to get sent home from the hospital after showing up too early. She practically wants to see the baby's head before going to the hospital, okay? So my wife is deep into labor while pregnant with Maranatha, and it's like ten o'clock at night. I know that between driving, checking in, getting to our room—and then, you know, her having to give birth—we're going to be up for a number of hours that will basically feel infinite. Which is fine, and beautiful, and amazing. I'm ready for it.

At the time, we lived in a town house, and our car was parked at the top of a steep hill. I'm in super-husband mode, so I go huffing up the hill to grab the car and drive it back down to our doorstep. My bride is about to have a baby, people—out of my way!

It's while I'm heading up to the car that one *tiny* little problem hits me: *Man, this is going to be a loooong night. We ate dinner at five. Dang, I'm hungry!*

I reach the car, start it up, drive it down to right in front of the door—a tiny bit faster than is safe, but remember: #superhusband—and then I leap out. I'm doing okay on the husband thing, but I realize I could go to the next level by cleaning out the car before my wife gets in.

But the backseat. Oh my goodness, there was so much food in it. Not real food, though. Toddler leftovers. Our oldest, Obadiah, was about three. We're talking enough food to feed ten squirrels for a hundred years, okay? So I start scraping Cheerios into piles with my hands, and collecting little bits of Goldfish and half-eaten peanut-butter-and-jelly sandwiches . . . and then time freezes.

The world becomes a single image. An artificially orange image.

Cheez-Its.

They're in a messy pile next to the car seat.

I'm in the valley of decision. It was as if everything hung in the balance.

Don't you eat those, Fusco. Don't do it.

I stare at them. My stomach growls. *You'll get into trouble. Do. Not. Do. It. Come on, Fusco, you know—*

But I can't hear myself anymore over the sound of chewing. The Cheez-Its are tasting like manna from heaven!

And before you get all judgy, I felt like I *needed* to eat. I wasn't going to turn to my wife on the way to the hospital and be like, "Honey, let's zip through the drive-through, okay?"

So I try to extract every bit of nutrition I can from those Cheez-Its. I'm really going for it. And then I grab a half-empty water bottle and sort of swish my mouth out, and use my fingernail to pick out my molars. Drop a mint in my mouth. Clean car, partially fed Daniel. Win-win, right?

I open the front door.

My wife is standing there, having a contraction. I rush to her side for support. Then through the pain, her eyes lock on mine. She looks unsure at first and then angry. Then she yells, "What are you *eating!*"

• • •

Why do I tell you such an embarrassing story? Partly because I know I'm gonna get some support from my fellow floor-of-the-car eaters. Amen?

And also because self-control is such an important part of life.

Self-control influences so many elements of a healthy life. Our diet, how hard we work, how we spend our money, the vices we choose to avoid, the people we spend time with, when we go to bed and wake up . . . the list is nearly endless. And all of us want to get better at either doing certain things or avoiding certain things.

Which makes me think we could all use some more self-control.

Self-control is our capacity to override unwanted thoughts, feelings, and impulses. And it has to do with delaying gratification. If we choose not to do something in the short term in order to meet a goal in the long term, then we're practicing a certain amount of self-control.

We can also call that willpower. We all have it, and we all use it. It's natural to focus on the times we *don't* use self-control, like when we eat that extra brownie or, I don't know, Cheez-Its off the floor of the car. But every day we use self-control in good ways, too, such as when we actually get out of bed when our alarm goes off.

The need for self-control is universally relevant. Not all of us struggle in every area, but all of us struggle in *some* area. The Bible helps us train in the area of self-control and increase the amount we have. We'll look at this later in the chapter, but let's just say there's a reason self-control is one of the fruits produced in our lives by God's Spirit.

God's basic promise is that if we deny something lesser to focus on him, he'll reward us with increased self-control.

Which is exactly what we long for, isn't it? That's the inward need in this chapter: our longing for self-control. It's not very sexy to talk about *longing* for self-control. Think about it. Have you ever said anything like this?

"I sure wish I could lose ten pounds, but I can't seem to
   stay motivated."
"Dang, it's so hard to resist buying things online even
   though I know I can't afford it."
"What would my life be like if I could stop doing this?"
"If only I could add that helpful habit to my life."

Here's where things get weird, though. Even weirder than
car Cheez-Its. Because I'm not going to say that we should
white-knuckle our way through life or crank up the willpower to eleven.

What I'm going to suggest goes against our DNA. Think
about what you see on TV when they show pictures of "typical Americans." We're number one in all kinds of terrible
stuff: diabetes per capita, total sugar consumed, number of
fast-food restaurants, and so on. We love to eat to the point
of harming ourselves. Which is why every shot of us on the
evening news is taken from the waist down, from behind,
and it's all junk-in-the-trunk and cankles, right?

And against that backdrop, I'm going to suggest that our
longing for self-control is satisfied, in part, by fasting.

Ouch.

But why bother? Because multiple studies have concluded
that lack of self-control or willpower is one of the biggest
barriers to change. When we want to do something good in
our lives and then we fail, it's most often because we can't
control ourselves.

I bet your experience confirms that. I know mine does!

Fortunately, God has a ton of good news for us about

fasting, and if we take it to heart, it's going to transform the way we think and live.

Promise

Fasting.

It's hard to think of a single word that will take the air out of a room faster. Heck, we'd rather pass the offering plate around a few more times than talk about fasting—let alone actually fast!

On the other hand, our Bibles are absolutely *packed* with references to fasting, which makes for some serious cognitive dissonance.

Let's start simple, then, with two definitions of fasting that are brilliant. Notice how they build on each other.

- "Fasting confirms our utter dependence upon God by finding in him a source of sustenance beyond food."[1]

- "Fasting, if we conceive of it truly, must not . . . be confined to the question of food and drink; fasting should really be made to include abstinence from anything which is legitimate in and of itself for the sake of some special spiritual purpose. There are many bodily functions which are right and normal and perfectly legitimate, but which for special peculiar reasons in certain circumstances should be controlled. That is fasting."[2]

---

[1] Dallas Willard, *The Spirit of the Disciplines: Understanding How God Changes Lives* (New York: HarperCollins, 1991), 166.

[2] D. Martyn Lloyd-Jones, *Studies in the Sermon on the Mount* (Grand Rapids, MI: Eerdmans, 1984), 38.

The first idea we may have heard before. We give up food, and it stinks for a while . . . but then, somehow, it gets better! We discover that "people don't live on food alone," to paraphrase Jesus. We learn that God can sustain and fill us and that we literally cannot experience certain elements of God's provision when our stomachs are full.

But then the second quote makes the first richer and fuller. If fasting from food is the bass line to our song, let's add in drums and piano. See, we can fast from almost *anything*. And when we do so for the right reasons, we'll be playing in harmony with God, and our minds are going to be blown!

Remember that we're connecting our *longing* for more self-control with the *practice* of fasting.

One reason we're hesitant to talk about fasting is that we lack enough self-control . . . or at least we *think* we do. But we've actually been practicing self-control our whole lives. It starts when we're young. If you're a parent, you know that potty training is all about the exercise of self-control. The child needs to go but will hold it until there's a toilet handy. We also teach our kids not to belch in restaurants or run across the street. And it keeps going into adulthood, when we control our urge to ram our car into that yellow Hummer that just stole our parking space.

This isn't fasting we're talking about, but these examples show how familiar we are with using self-control to make life better in the long run.

Fasting takes that same idea and applies it specifically to our relationship with God.

See, in a world full of temptations, a world where our

lack of self-control is easily evident, fasting helps us learn to choose God over everything else. Fasting trains us to make sure our decisions reflect who we really are, not who the world wants us to be. We learn to love ourselves properly by living with God, according to God's daily invitation. Fasting helps us see that this kind of life is only possible when we chose God's best for ourselves.

Fast Privately, but Do Fast

Jesus spirituality looks to Jesus to lead us into the street-level—yet heaven-bound—way of living. And because Jesus loved to speak about fasting, we should probably pay attention to that. So let's read our first scripture for this chapter:

> When you fast, do not look somber as the hypocrites
> do, for they disfigure their faces to show others
> they are fasting. Truly I tell you, they have received
> their reward in full. But when you fast, put oil on
> your head and wash your face, so that it will not be
> obvious to others that you are fasting, but only to
> your Father, who is unseen; and your Father, who
> sees what is done in secret, will reward you.[3]

That's Jesus, talking to his disciples and also to a whole bunch of strangers who are listening. And it's really important that we understand the background here—both what Jesus' Bible (the Old Testament) taught about fasting and how the pastors and religious professors of

---

3 Matthew 6:16-18.

his day fasted. Looking at only Old Testament examples, fasting was

- for remembrance,[4]
- for confession,[5]
- for expressing humiliation and contrition,[6]
- for grieving or bereavement,[7] and
- even done out of desperation or anguish.[8]

So we're talking about a very godly and *very* multipurpose activity! Unfortunately, the Pharisees of Jesus' day had perfected an unapproved use, pioneered by the Israelites hundreds of years earlier: prideful hypocrisy.

The religious bigwigs of Jesus' day were fasting *all the time*. Trouble is, they were going around like a bunch of moaning zombies, just to make sure that everybody knew how holy they were.

That's why Jesus tells us to clean up real nice when we're fasting and to act as we normally act when we're not fasting. That way, the fast will be between us and God, not us and other people. Don't forget, Jesus' culture was very different from ours. His was steeped in religion and religious practices. Things like tithing and prayer and fasting were part of the rhythm of everyday public life. And because life was religiously charged, certain people wanted to stand out. They wanted everyone to notice how holy they were.

---

4 Zechariah 7:3-5; 8:19.

5 Nehemiah 9:1-2; Psalm 35:13; Isaiah 58:3, 5; Daniel 9:2-20; 10:2-3; Jonah 3:5.

6 Leviticus 16:29-34; 23:26-32; Numbers 29:7-11; Deuteronomy 9:18; 1 Kings 21:27; Nehemiah 9:1; Daniel 9:3, 4; Jonah 3:5.

7 1 Samuel 31:13; 1 Chronicles 10:11, 12; 2 Samuel 1:12.

8 Exodus 24:18; Judges 20:26; 2 Samuel 1:12; 2 Chronicles 20:3; Ezra 8:21-23; Esther 4:16.

That does not describe our culture, I realize. If you go to Starbucks and order a small water[9] and then grab your stomach and groan, no one is going to think you're a holy roller.

But we need to be careful about this *within* our churches. Here's a not-so-funny funny story about that.

When I was first starting out, there was this local pastor who decided, "I'm going to fast for forty days and forty nights."

You could say he was following Jesus, since he was doing the same fast. Except he was ignoring the teaching of Jesus, because everybody—and I mean *everybody*—knew he was fasting!

He'd be at something like a local pastor's breakfast, where there's this buffet with some eggs and bacon and cinnamon rolls—the works. And while everyone else was loading up their plates, he would just kind of shuffle through the line, clutching his sad little plastic water bottle.

You know what some people said?

"God is going to bless his church *so much!*"

Six months later the church closed down. Everybody left.

Now I'm not saying this is cause and effect. But the deal with fasting is this: An ostentatious *display* of your fasting will always kill the fast. You might still be refraining from something, but your fast is over. At the point when you let everyone know about it, it's a fast in name only.

I might go so far as to say that if anyone—maybe not counting your spouse or best friend or pastor—knows you're fasting . . . then you're not really fasting.

---

9 Oops, I mean a "tall" water.

So when you fast, keep it to yourself! Check out what Jesus says: The people who are fasting the wrong way are the posers and pretenders. And they *are* rewarded. They get noticed. They get brownie points for being so "spiritual."

But that's *all* they get.

They don't get the thing they're really longing for. What all of us are longing for. A deeper, clearer connection to God the Father. An experience of increasing self-control, through God's Spirit, that can bring clarity and blessing. That *only* happens when we fast in private.

Which leads us to a second, extremely short point from this scripture.

Ready? The second point (blink and you'll miss it) is that you need to fast!

Look what Jesus says: "When you fast . . . " "But when you fast . . . " Jesus is *assuming* his followers will fast, *just as he does*.

Now if Jesus assumes we're going to do something, and he tells us how to do it the right way . . . I don't know about you, but I'm going to move that out of the "optional" column in my Christian life!

Fast for the Right Reasons

Jesus assumes his followers are going too fast. He tells us to keep it private.[10] And to do it for the right reasons.

We also know that fasting isn't limited to food. Rather,

---

[10] Ever notice that being ostentatious about spirituality is always a temptation? Picture a pastor who answers any compliment with a pious nod to the heavens, saying, "Oh, it's not *me* . . . it's God!" Or the athlete who scores a touchdown, points to the sky in humble gratitude toward God . . . and then kisses his own bicep. We're amazing at taking pride and figuring out how to wrap it up in spiritual stuff!

it's exercising godly self-control over some area of life for a spiritual purpose. Like when Jesus wakes up before dawn and heads into the hills (see Mark 1:35 for one of many examples), that's fasting. Jesus is setting aside something good—sleep!—for a certain purpose.

So let's take a closer look at the purpose of fasting, using a beautiful passage from the prophet Isaiah. The passage is a bit long, so let me give you the point right at the start: We don't fast to "get" something from God but rather to *hear his voice* and to *give*.

Here's what Isaiah says in chapter 58:

> Shout it aloud, do not hold back.
>   Raise your voice like a trumpet.
> Declare to my people their rebellion
>   and to the descendants of Jacob their sins.
> For day after day they seek me out;
>   they seem eager to know my ways,
> as if they were a nation that does what is right
>   and has not forsaken the commands of its God.
> They ask me for just decisions
>   and seem eager for God to come near them.
> "Why have we fasted," they say,
>   "and you have not seen it?
> Why have we humbled ourselves,
>   and you have not noticed?"
>
> Yet on the day of your fasting, you do as you please
>   and exploit all your workers.

Your fasting ends in quarreling and strife,
    and in striking each other with wicked fists.
You cannot fast as you do today
    and expect your voice to be heard on high.
Is this the kind of fast I have chosen,
    only a day for people to humble themselves?
Is it only for bowing one's head like a reed
    and for lying in sackcloth and ashes?
Is that what you call a fast,
    a day acceptable to the LORD?

Is not this the kind of fasting I have chosen:
to loose the chains of injustice
    and untie the cords of the yoke,
to set the oppressed free
    and break every yoke?
Is it not to share your food with the hungry
    and to provide the poor wanderer with shelter—
when you see the naked, to clothe them,
    and not to turn away from your own flesh and blood?
Then your light will break forth like the dawn,
    and your healing will quickly appear;
then your righteousness will go before you,
    and the glory of the LORD will be your rear guard.
Then you will call, and the LORD will answer;
    you will cry for help, and he will say: Here am I.

If you do away with the yoke of oppression,
    with the pointing finger and malicious talk,

and if you spend yourselves in behalf of the hungry
    and satisfy the needs of the oppressed,
then your light will rise in the darkness,
    and your night will become like the noonday.
The LORD will guide you always;
    he will satisfy your needs in a sun-scorched land
    and will strengthen your frame.
You will be like a well-watered garden,
    like a spring whose waters never fail.[11]

That passage is so great. And clear! Part of me wants to leave it there.

(Another part of me is the guy who preaches hour-long sermons, so let's keep going for a few pages.)

First thing we notice is that fasting isn't a way to strong-arm God into giving us something. That's exactly what the Israelites in this passage were trying. In verse 3 they ask God, "Hey, why aren't you paying attention to how awesome we're fasting? When you see that, you're supposed to pay us back!"

Basically, the Israelites are trying to do something good for God *in order to put God in their debt.* Sounds kind of crazy when we see it written out like that, but don't we try to pull the same stunt today?

I meet people all the time who are like, "Sorry, Pastor, but I don't follow Jesus anymore. I used to, and I did everything I was supposed to, but God never gave me what I wanted!"

I'm like, "That's not following Jesus—that's trying to *use* Jesus as a vending machine!"

---

[11] Isaiah 58:1-11.

What God tells the Israelites in this passage is that they're getting the externals right, but their motivation is all wrong . . . which eventually leads to wrong externals as well! Their fast is divorced from real life. In fact, *while* they're fasting, they're simultaneously exploiting their workers!

God's after something better than just "sackcloth and ashes." He wants changed hearts, which lead to changed lives—our lives *and* the lives of others.

Hearing God

As we've talked about, fasting doesn't get us something *from* God, but it does get us closer *to* God. And when we're closer to God, it's easier to listen for his voice. Fasting dials down the background noise so we can focus and hear.

Let's look at Isaiah again:

> Then your light will break forth like the dawn,
>   and your healing will quickly appear;
> then your righteousness will go before you,
>   and the glory of the LORD will be your rear
>   guard.
> Then you will call, and the LORD will answer;
>   you will cry for help, and he will say: Here am I.[12]

Sounds great, right? Now, we'll remember from what we read in the rest of the passage that there are some very important things surrounding those verses, and we'll get into that

---

[12] Isaiah 58:8-9.

next. But first I want us to sit with this idea of hearing God, because it's a big deal. Fasting gets us to a unique place in our relationship with God.

On my first fast, I didn't understand that right away. In fact, I'll never forget the clear feeling I immediately received.

It was grumpiness!

I don't think I'd ever skipped a meal on purpose in my life. I tried a nap. I tried playing my bass. But man, my blood sugar was bottomed out. I took the worst nap ever and woke up all cranky.

To be honest, I couldn't handle life without food.

And then . . . I could!

There's this initial barrier, for sure, but on the other side we find something waiting—something other than grumpiness.

I started journaling and reading my Bible. I wasn't hungry. I wasn't grumpy. And all of a sudden I felt God speaking to my heart. I feel comfortable saying that because, for one, I don't say it that often and also because I remember exactly what God let me know.

Daniel, music is your love and your passion. I've given you that gift. But I don't want music to be your primary ministry. I've called you to the ministry of the Word.

So I wrote—and I still have this journal by the way—"I've been called to the ministry of the Word."

I had never experienced that unique type of clarity before. Fasting pushed me closer to God . . . close enough to hear his voice! Fasting meant I was listening when God was ready to speak.

And remember how God spoke to me about ministry? Well, that brings us back to the surrounding verses from Isaiah. Because that promise of personally hearing God leads to something vital we can't afford to miss: God speaks to us inwardly so that he can lead us outward!

BLESSING OTHERS

Don't miss this: Fasting takes us *in* so we can go *up* and so we can be sent *out*.

We choose to give up something that we regularly do or enjoy. Whatever your thing is—eating the kids' Halloween candy, one-click buying on Amazon, shouting at people—*whatever* your thing is, fasting is how God turns that around so that you can listen to him. Once we start listening, we hear how he wants the Kingdom to look. And God's Spirit grows the self-control in us, through fasting, that we'll need to live outward and bless the world in the name of Jesus.

Look at verses 6 and 7 again:

> Is not this the kind of fasting I have chosen:
> to loose the chains of injustice
>   and untie the cords of the yoke,
> to set the oppressed free
>   and break every yoke?
> Is it not to share your food with the hungry
>   and to provide the poor wanderer with shelter—
> when you see the naked, to clothe them,

and not to turn away from your own flesh and
blood?

Fasting leads to blessing others. Let me say that again because it's so important: *Fasting leads to blessing others.*

It's easy to see how the food part of that works. The less we eat, the more there is for others. A person can fast from lunch every day for a month and keep that food in their pantry, right? But that person can also share that food with people who are hungry! The connection is just as strong with nonfood fasting. The less we use our words to cause bitterness and strife, the more grace and forgiveness can enter broken lives. The less we watch reruns of *Seinfeld* late at night, the more we can pray and intercede for others.[13]

If you've ever wondered *why* you are part of this world, here's God's answer: You've been put into this world in the name of Jesus so that the world may be changed by the presence of Jesus in you.

Good old-fashioned willpower has a decent chance of getting you the American dream or at least a taste of it.

God's dream for us is infinitely bigger than the American dream. It takes much more than willpower. It takes Spirit power.

We've been talking throughout this whole book about the art of living. Jesus spirituality. And a big part of that is learning how to steward our lives for the maximum impact on God's Kingdom. If we want to have maximum impact, we

---

[13] What's cool is that this stuff Isaiah talks about is exactly what Jesus uses as his mission statement when he launches his ministry. It's also how Jesus describes separating the sheep from the goats at Judgment Day. Read the beginning of Luke 4 and the last part of Matthew 25 for extra credit and a gold star!

can't be content to "use some willpower" every so often when we need to get things done.

Instead, we need to tell God we want to learn the self-control that's waiting for us. Let's not allow our religion to get in the way of what God wants to do inside us, through fasting. And I promise you this: Whatever God wants to do, it will benefit us, *and* those around us, in amazing ways.

Fasting is stepping off the moment and stepping into eternity. What would happen if, through fasting, you stepped into the plans and purposes that God has for you?

Practice

🔁 Let's start with some **types of fasting**.

🔁 There are literally a million different ways.[14] Take anything you do regularly. Anything. You can fast from eating. (Not from hydration, by the way—Jesus certainly hydrated during his fasting. The human body shuts down and dies after several days without water.) You can fast from meat or fancy foods. You can fast from media. You can fast from a meal, or two meals, a day. You can fast from electronics. You can fast from music or radio. It doesn't matter what, as long as it's something that's a normal part of your life and you're willing to give it up for a certain amount of time.

🔁 Maybe a bunch of your coworkers are against God and say negative things about Christians. So one day a week

---

[14] My copyeditor strongly encouraged me to change this sentence. Some people are *literally* as prickly as a porcupine when it comes to grammar stuff like that!

you leave your food at home and during your lunch hour you take a prayer walk. The important thing is that you:

- Privately set something aside

- Take that time to focus on God

Take an inventory of the areas in which you struggle with self-control.

Would one of those be a wise area to fast and to allow God to satisfy your need for self-control?

As you make fasting a regular part of your life, **be considerate of others**.

If you're fasting from food and someone offers you a piece of homemade cake at a party, eat it! Don't make that person feel bad, and don't announce your fast to others. Remember, God sees what is done in private. If you're truly fasting, then there's only one person who truly needs to know. And who knows, you might just get some dessert out of the deal.

intentionality / biblical simplicity

Problem

Intentionality is a popular concept in our culture right now.

We're invited to be intentional about pretty much everything. How we exercise and spend our time. What we do with our money. How we speak and think. What kind of food we eat, where we buy that food, and where that food was grown and who grew it.

Intentionality can be a good thing. But when I look back over my life, it's clear that not all intentions are created equal.

During my first year of college, for example, I was one of the most intentional people in history. Seriously. Everything I did was motivated by a single goal. I structured my classes around that desire. I changed the way I slept and ate and studied. As we talked about in the last chapter, I used self-control to say no to certain things so that I could say yes to the thing that really mattered to me.

Which just so happened to be partying.

But still. I was intentional!

It wasn't until the first few weeks of my second year that I realized there was *no* amount of partying that could make me feel happy and fulfilled. Over and over it was the same story: happy for a few hours, distracted for a few hours, then a hollow feeling . . . which led me to chase the next party.

So I said to myself, with all the wisdom of a nineteen-year-old, "This is *not* working—and I've been partying like a rock star for, like, a *long* time."

Well, what else could I try? I knew I loved music. I'd been playing in bands for a few years already, ever since I picked up my first bass back in middle school. So I decided to be intentional about something else: becoming a nasty bass player.

First step was to set my alarm for 6:00 a.m. every day. Which was funny, because my roommate at the time was still living the classic college lifestyle where his earliest classes started at 3:00 p.m., since he liked to go to *bed* around 6:00 a.m. We were a tag team: My alarm to get up was his cue to go to sleep. I'd stumble out of bed, high-five him, and while he was getting cozy in his bed, I'd plug into my amp, put my headphones on, and start practicing.

I was incredibly intentional about that pursuit. I got pretty good at playing bass. And it was a way better thing to be intentional about than partying.

But it's not like playing bass all the time was an existential cure. Although I loved it, and still love it to this day, it didn't satisfy my soul. So I kept looking. I was hoping to find something to focus my intentionality on that would be *the* thing.

Have you ever felt like that? As though you'd be happy to focus your life on something, if only you knew what? Life has never been more fragmented and frantic. There are countless things clamoring for our attention. And make no mistake . . . we're *always* intentionally pursuing *something*.

Our intentions shape our lives. Which means that if we intend the wrong things, or trivial things, we'll never live the lives God created us for.

Promise

We all know who Albert Einstein is: the guy who started that chain of bagel shops. He believed that "everything should be made as simple as possible, but not simpler."[1] Because right on the other side of simple is simplistic. *Too* simple. Overly simple to the point of harm.

In light of that, I want to give you one thing in this chapter. Just one! If you grab on to this, by the Holy Spirit and because of the finished work of Jesus, I promise you'll discover something simple enough and deep enough to last a lifetime. We find it in our scripture for this chapter, Matthew 6:33-34:

> Seek first his kingdom and his righteousness, and all
> these things will be given to you as well. Therefore
> do not worry about tomorrow, for tomorrow will

---

[1] "Albert Einstein Quotes," BrainyQuote, https://www.brainyquote.com/quotes/quotes/a /alberteins103652.html.

worry about itself. Each day has enough trouble of its own.

Like a small spring that taps into a deep well of cold, clean water, the message in these two verses is basically an inexhaustible source of teaching for our lives. Simple, but never simplistic.

Okay, so here's our one main point: *Biblical simplicity is intentionally prioritizing God's Kingdom.*

Boom. That's really the heart of the art of living right there, so it's fitting we find it at the heart of our book.

This simple teaching is so vital that we need to hear it over and over and over! *Prioritize God's Kingdom.* We need that every day or three times a day. We need to set our phones to remind us every hour on the hour. *Prioritize God's Kingdom.*

All right, I'm smart enough to know that I've run us smack into a cultural minefield here. This might be a one-point chapter, but that point needs a bit of explaining.

To start with, we're ambivalent about the whole kingdom/king thing.

On the one hand, we're suspicious of kings. America was founded by folks who wanted to represent themselves, rather than having to listen to some distant ruler. We have a separation of powers in our government because we want to be as sure as possible that one knucklehead—or a small group of knuckleheads—can't ruin everything.[2]

But on the other hand, we want to *be* kings—at least of

---

[2] If we manage to fill all *three* branches of government with knuckleheads, then all bets are off—but that's a discussion for another day!

our own little kingdoms. We figure we'll get it right if given the chance.

Our suspicion about kings isn't a major deal. I can imagine someone saying, "I refuse to follow *any* authority other than myself!" That attitude would be the subject of its own chapter—or better yet, its own conversation! But for the rest of us, who are either following Jesus or who want to be following Jesus, we're willing to admit that God's kingship is in a class by itself. Earthly kings, and rulers of all types, screw up. Like, constantly. But God is the King of kings. And unlike human rulers, God always acts in a way that is perfect, loving, just, and benevolent. God is the perfect king, which means God is the *only* king we can actually trust, 100 percent, without getting burned.

Our desire to *be* kings, though, causes all sorts of problems! In fact, we're going to spend the rest of the chapter looking at them. A king is responsible for at least three things in his kingdom:

1. The people's priorities
2. The people's unity
3. The people's provision

And what we'll see is that while human rulers more or less fail at all three, God shows us the perfect way to live intentionally. Biblical simplicity is about accomplishing the most important things, and these three realities teach us what God sees as important. If we want to live in godly simplicity, we have to start here.

Priorities

For some reason we seem predisposed to want everyone *else* to do things *our* way, even when it doesn't make sense. No matter how important or how insignificant the issue, we manage to convince ourselves that we're right. What we want is to take the priorities of our own small kingdoms and apply them to all of life.

Here's an easy example that pops up in the church: music preferences.

At church you throw together people, sometimes by the hundreds or thousands, who all love Jesus and who all love *totally* different music.

So as a pastor, I'll have someone pull me aside and tell me, with passion in their voice, that the music is simply too loud. What I don't say back is that earlier in the day, someone told me with passion in *their* voice that the music was too quiet!

I've heard complaints about the worship leader wearing a hat. Or not wearing one. Or that there were too many guitars. Or no guitars. Or that it was so loud or slow or soft or fast or long or spontaneous or brief or planned. Probably eight or nine out of every ten comments we get about our service have to do with the music.

Look, church was God's idea. We're commanded to keep gathering together. So God's reason for church must not be about making everybody happy, because that's clearly impossible!

There will always be people more focused on their own kingdoms than on God's Kingdom. Sometimes that's as simple as making something like musical preference a Big Deal. But when we prioritize God's Kingdom, we realize something: *The music style doesn't flippin' matter!* Why? Because God is our king, and God is glorious and worthy of praise, and there isn't just one style of music or worship that conveys that.

We cannot let our preferences and priorities become ultimate.

Unlike our priorities, the priorities of God's Kingdom never change—plus they're always perfect.

In God's Kingdom, the priorities are the same. To restore us to a right relationship with him. To bring glory to God's name. To cast out fear with perfect love. To put an ultimate end to evil. To bring a new and everlasting Kingdom. And the ultimate priority? Look to the Cross. God is not willing that any should be lost. Rather, he wants to bring us back from our rebellion, even at the cost of his Son's life.

The King's priorities need to be the priorities of the people. Prioritizing God's Kingdom means asking God what he wants to do, learning what he wants to do, and making it our primary goal to partner with that. Not with what *we* think is best, but with God's priorities.

Real quick, if you've been following Jesus for a long time, I need to tell you something.

There's a temptation to think, *I've been coming to church every week since I was a kid. The church is my life. So maybe I'll skip this chapter, because I'm* already *prioritizing God's Kingdom.*

Don't make that mistake.

The length of time you've been a Christian does not correlate with whether you're prioritizing God's Kingdom.

Am I suggesting that if you've been going to church since the carpet was shagged and the songs were all on overhead projectors,[3] you're a Pharisee? Not a bit! But going to church that long doesn't automatically make you someone whose life revolves around God's Kingdom either.

Here's an example of how, even after decades in church, our priorities can fail to match up with the King's. Think back over the last month. How many times did you hang out with a fellow believer, and how many times did you hang out with an unbeliever? How many times did you have a real conversation with a stranger, or someone in a different socioeconomic bracket, or someone from a different culture?

How often do you do things, out of love, that would get you into trouble at your church?

That's how Jesus acted *all the time*. And his entire life was about prioritizing God's Kingdom.

Prioritizing God's Kingdom means we value what God values. Jesus didn't start a church and then attend it fifty-two Sabbaths a year, plus prayer meetings and potlucks. So if we have no friends who are unbelievers? If we never speak with homeless people? If we're disgusted by and turn away from people living sinful lifestyles?

Then we're not prioritizing God's Kingdom.

Just like if we're concerned with our own limited priorities, we're not prioritizing God's Kingdom.

Henry David Thoreau said, "Our life is frittered away by detail."[4] He wrote that in the mid-nineteenth century, but

---

3 Or—gasp—printed in actual hymnbooks!
4 Henry David Thoreau, *The Portable Thoreau* (New York: Penguin, 2012), 271.

it sounds like he's talking about today. See, one of our major problems with prioritizing God's Kingdom is that we try to make his Kingdom *one* of our priorities. We tack it on to our list.

But God will not be tacked on. It just doesn't work that way. Either we're letting the King set our priorities, or we're not. Either we seek first God's Kingdom, or we seek first our own. This beautiful intentionality of prioritizing what God asks us to makes things simple.

When we prioritize God's Kingdom, though, his righteousness becomes the driving ethics for our lives. What happens is that God teaches us, by his own actions, how we're supposed to live and move and have our being.

We simply weren't created to be the kings and queens of our own lives. When we try, we're trying to catch the wind in our hands.

Some of you will be thinking, *You don't know me, Fusco. I am good enough and strong enough to be the ruler of my own life. My own kingdom is the place I want to live and die, thank you very much.*

I hear stuff like that all the time. And I've got two responses.

One, you might be right . . . for now. For another day or week or year. You might not notice your insufficiency. Yet.

Two, you *say* I don't know you—out of pride or defensiveness or fear—but deep down you know I'm right. Pretend otherwise, say otherwise, but you know at the core of who you are that living for your own kingdom, for your own priorities, is antithetical to your truest self.

God's the only king with the right priorities. *Perfect* priorities.

We're the subjects of that perfect king, and we follow his lead.

Unity

God's priorities are the ones that will build God's Kingdom.

Another way of saying that—and get excited, because this is a *seriously* short section—is that God's priorities are the only ones that can unite a broken world. Human priorities inevitably divide, while God's priorities bring people together, and all of us together with God.

Let that sink in for a moment. God wants to heal a broken world and bring unity. Talk about an elegant simplicity! God's plan is for Jesus to bring people, with every conceivable type of diversity, into *one* family!

That's so different from the hurting, complicated world we humans have made. While I was writing this book, individuals *claiming* to be following God's priorities chose to use automatic rifles and bombs to kill 130 civilians in Paris. And the attackers said God told them to do it. God didn't tell them that. God wouldn't tell them that.[5] So don't get sidetracked here and say, "Religion is what divides the world." Because we're talking about God here, not what some people claim in the name of God.

I probably don't need to convince you that our priorities are what break the world in the first place. When we

---

5 "IS Claims Paris Attacks, Warns Operation Is 'First of the Storm,'" SITE Intelligence Group, November 14, 2015, https://ent.siteintelgroup.com/Statements/is-claims-paris-attacks-warns-operation-is-first-of-the -storm.html.

prioritize the kingdom of self (which is highly fortified, by the way), every relationship that is not serving *our* kingdom is fractured and compromised. Families rip apart, friendships rip apart, and communities rip apart whenever we focus on the reign of self.

As the kings of our own little castles, we can bring to the table only what we own. Our values, our strengths, our skills. Thing is, we bring the inevitable flip side as well. Our insecurities and hang-ups. Our failures. Our shame.

That's not a recipe for lasting unity!

Look at this picture of what true unity looks like, when it flows from God's priorities:

> For this reason, since the day we heard about you, we have not stopped praying for you. We continually ask God to fill you with the knowledge of his will through all the wisdom and understanding that the Spirit gives, so that you may live a life worthy of the Lord and please him in every way: bearing fruit in every good work, growing in the knowledge of God, being strengthened with all power according to his glorious might so that you may have great endurance and patience, and giving joyful thanks to the Father, who has qualified you to share in the inheritance of his holy people in the kingdom of light. For he has rescued us from the dominion of darkness and brought us into the kingdom of the Son he loves, in whom we have redemption, the forgiveness of sins.[6]

---

[6] Colossians 1:9-14.

Now *that's* lasting unity. Unity that depends on God's love and leading, not our own efforts.

Unfortunately, we're more likely to break the very things we try to fix.

But fortunately, God is the opposite. Isaiah 42:3 tells us that God is able to restore even the most fragile, damaged life. That's the kind of unity we need, the kind of unity our hurting world needs, and the kind of unity that comes only from a perfect king.

Provision

So far we have a King—the *right* kind of king—who provides us with the only priorities capable of satisfying us and uniting a broken world.

That isn't the only thing God provides, though. In fact, when we prioritize God's Kingdom, God provides *everything* we need.

Read our scripture one more time:

Seek first his kingdom and his righteousness, and all these things will be given to you as well. Therefore do not worry about tomorrow, for tomorrow will worry about itself. Each day has enough trouble of its own.

If we prioritize God's Kingdom, *then* we will trust God's provision. That's how it works.

Don't let this truth pass by unnoticed. For many of us, our lack of simplicity is directly linked to our anxiety over provision. We feel completely on the hook to be responsible for everything. This anxiety robs our lives of the very intentionality we know we need.

If we prioritize God's Kingdom, though, we will also trust God's provision.

We've got to read this in context. (As I like to say, if you take a text out of context, all you're left with is a con.) Starting in verse 25, Jesus is more or less telling everyone, "Don't worry, don't worry, don't worry." Not about what you'll eat, not about what you'll wear, not about where you'll live. Those are the most basic parts of life, the necessities, and Jesus is telling us not to worry about them. It seems crazy.

And it would be, if it wasn't the King of kings talking.

Remember, when we're in charge of our own kingdoms, *we* are the ones in charge of taking care of ourselves. That's exactly what keeps many of us from truly prioritizing God's Kingdom and truly trusting. We're afraid that if we stop controlling everything, the careful little kingdoms we've constructed will crumble.

Take my dad. He worked for decades to take care of my mom, my sisters, and me. And now that he's living on his retirement savings, know what his biggest fear is? Outliving his money. A ton of us worry about that, and the numbers are only growing as Americans live longer and longer.

I don't mean to minimize this fear. I don't think I am, actually. But outliving your money is only a big fear if providing for your life is completely dependent on you, right? Whereas in God's Kingdom, the King has infinite resources. Inexhaustible resources!

Think about it like this: No matter how carefully you save and plan, no matter how careful and self-sufficient you are, *you can still lose everything*. Depressing, right?

Here's a scary thought: Maybe God wants us to outlive our money. Why? Well, what if he wants to use us in new and fruitful ways . . . but first he needs to teach us that we don't need our own provision, but rather the provision that comes from our heavenly Father?

Some of you are saying, "You've gone too far, Fusco. You're telling people to chuck their retirement plans and sell their houses *in case* God wants to teach them something . . . but you're going to cause a lot of people a lot of pain!"

First, I'm not a financial adviser, okay? I'm not *telling* you to do anything in particular with your money. Second, though, I'm pretty sure we're getting enough advice from the other side! I doubt we need to be told to save *more*, to plan ahead *more*, to worry *more*. Our "economy" is actually only a *slice* of the total economy of life. The economy we talk about is a goods-and-services economy. An economy of money and capital and stocks and savings. But God's economy includes resources that never show up in the *Wall Street Journal*—and it's an economy of abundance!

God doesn't want to make you healthy, wealthy, and wise—that's Benjamin Franklin! What God wants is to make you into the image of his Son, by the power of his Spirit.

God wants you to prioritize his Kingdom and trust him to provide as you do that.

Now since we're human, it's almost automatic for us to go from inexhaustible resources to asking God for a Mercedes for Christmas and a vacation home, right? (Or if we already have those things, for a private jet for Christmas and a second vacation home. And so on.) God promises to provide for our needs, though. Not our wants. Not even our "really been wanting it for a long time" wants.

Unfortunately, if we don't guard our lives with a holy simplicity, we begin to love ourselves in some really funky ways! Ways that rob us of the most important things. We begin to covet. We begin to rack up debt for things that don't even satisfy. And we begin to seek after other, lesser kingdoms.

No one needs the latest video-game console. No one needs the latest smartphone—or even a smartphone that's a few years old. No one needs a new car or a new house or a new boyfriend or a new Fender bass guitar.

Might we *want* those things? Totally. (Especially the bass!) But God never promises to give us everything we want. And for good reason! Lots of the stuff we want would be bad for us. Worse, it would be bad for others.

But here's the amazing part: When we prioritize God's Kingdom, we get better and better at telling the difference between what we need and want. And what's even more amazing is that the better we get at telling the difference, the less we want what we used to want!

That's what it means to trust in God's provision.

Focus on God's Present

God is the King of kings—and that's a good thing! God gives us only the priorities that will satisfy us. Priorities that unite rather than divide. Priorities that show us God's provision for our needs is absolutely dependable.

What that leads to is embracing God's present moment.

None of us know what tomorrow will bring, or even if we'll be alive tomorrow. "Do not worry about tomorrow, for tomorrow will worry about itself. Each day has enough trouble of its own." But God has given us today, along with everything we *need* today.

Maybe you're familiar with the verse that says, "Because of the LORD's great love we are not consumed, for his compassions never fail. They are new every morning; great is your faithfulness."[7]

That sounds almost . . . cheesy. Like a greeting card or a bumper sticker. But when you think about it, God's being street level with us. Completely realistic. God's like, "Today might be hard. It might suck. It *might* be amazing. Either way, I'm going to give you exactly what you need. I'm going to be with you and get you through to tomorrow . . . and then we're going to do it all over again."

And we're like, "That's cool, God. But . . . not sure how to ask this . . . could you give me *tomorrow's* needs today? Because what I'm worried about is—"

God cuts us off. "Buh-buh-buh. *Today.* We're taking this one day at a time. That's what you can handle. And that's what drives you back to me every time the sun rises."

The biblical truth is that if you worry about tomorrow, you'll miss today.

---

7 Lamentations 3:22-23.

How many times have you worried about something that never happened? Worrying is a bad investment!

The way we bear fruit—the fruit of the Spirit!—is to abide in God, day after day, step by step. God's grace is sufficient for whatever happens, but God gives us that grace *as* stuff happens. The King has infinite resources, remember, but we're not given them all at once. We're given them as we need them.

God has placed us here, right now, for this very moment.

God's care and provision are assured, but that does not mean life will be one long picnic. Rather, God's presence asks us to believe two simultaneous truths: *We will have trouble, and we will be taken care of.*

I don't have to convince you that there's darkness out there. God's Word calls us to be light. Like a city on a hill, shining like a welcome beacon to weary and hurting travelers. Shining like the dawn, guiding people's feet onto a path of shalom rather than a path of sin and shame.

Deep in your heart you're tired of prioritizing your own kingdom. Tired of feeling empty over and over. This isn't a small thing. We're talking about your life, your truest self. The *you* that Jesus died and rose again for.

We're talking about a new kingdom, with a perfectly loving King, where you can finally become who you are meant to be.

But to walk this way we must find ourselves walking in simplicity. We must live intentionally to make sure we pursue the most important things. There is nothing worse than succeeding in everything trivial and leaving the most important things undone. So let's simplify our lives!

Practice

- Make a list of things you prioritize, from big to small. Think about what you spend your time, your money, and your thoughts on. Think about what you plan for and dream about.

- What in that list takes you away from God's priorities?

- What in that list lines up with God's priorities?

- Is there anything in your life that you need to move from the Need column to the Want column?

- What do you currently find yourself living intentionally for?

- What would a simple and elegant Christian life look like?

- What do you worry about the most? What would it look like to start trusting God with these fears?

- Make an action plan to accomplish three things (even if they're small) each day that link up with God's priorities. Chart your success.

2.4

humility / direction

Problem

Let's make sure we know where we are.

We've reached the final chapter in our second movement: inward. As we look at Jesus spirituality and how to live the greatest commandment, we're moving upward, inward, and outward.

We've seen that living upward is essential and sets the pace for our lives. We worship, pray, deepen, and find stillness to grow in our experience of God's love. Then we move inward. Learning how God's love shapes our love for ourselves. We have already seen the need for confession, fasting, and simplicity.

Now that we're at our final inward need, you'll see there's

a good reason we saved it for last. Namely, because most people wouldn't agree it's even a need!

At least not at first. I'm counting on the fact that if you're still reading at this point, you're still willing to listen.

And my contention in this chapter is that all of us have a longing, often buried or unconscious, for humility. Not only that, but that longing is satisfied only when we are being directed and guided by someone wiser than we are.

Tough sell, I know.

There's a funny dynamic here. When it comes to other people, we *love* the idea of mentors and spiritual guides. Think Yoda and Luke. Ray Charles and Quincy Jones. Professor Dumbledore and Harry Potter. Usher and Justin Bieber.

When it comes to ourselves, though? *We* don't need mentors! Sure, we'd like to get better at certain things. We'd like to be more awesome and more admired. But mentors require honesty from us, and change takes time. Never mind that whole process. We're good the way we are—or at least good enough.

The problem is even worse with spiritual directors. A mentor at work is one thing. Or a mentor at CrossFit. We can compartmentalize that stuff. But giving someone access to our spiritual lives? We'd rather leave that for some dusty saint. We'll keep showing up at church and tithing and being good Christians. No need to get crazy.

But remember the question that started this whole investigation of the art of living: What's the most important commandment?

In other words, what's the *one* thing I should focus on? That's a human question in both a good and a bad way.

It's good because it shows the questioner wants to do the right thing. But it's also kind of sneaky! Because it's almost like the question is really "What's the *least* I can do and still have God think I'm a good person?"

Most of us do that all the time. We look for ways to downplay how much we really need to do spiritually.

Of course Jesus follows his usual method of exploding the question—and the heart—of the asker. Of us.

He *does* answer the question with a simple, two-part statement. It's just that the simple answer has implications for how we act, think, speak, work, pray, relax, and so on—24-7.

So . . . no big deal, really.

In all seriousness, though, that's why we need biblical humility. And it's why we each need a spiritual director to meet us inside that humility and help us stay focused on Jesus as we live upward, inward, and outward. Because if left to our own direction, we'd miss out on what Jesus wants for the fullness of our lives—on everything he wants to transform in us.

See, when Jesus saves people, he doesn't transform everything about their lives in one instant. Things take time. And conflict!

I knew that as a kid, long before I met Jesus. If you grow up all Italian in New Jersey, sarcasm is a love language. When someone loves you, they pick on you relentlessly. And man, I was the king of sarcasm.

Now when I came to know Jesus, I was not immediately convicted of my sarcasm, let alone cured of it. I was sarcastic to the core. Like I couldn't go two minutes without ripping on someone. In love, of course, but still. If I knew someone had a button I could push, I would push it relentlessly. *Tap-tap-tap-tap-tap*, like someone on their third energy drink of the morning.

But in the process of using my love language, I also hurt many people. I have a sad memory of making my friend Sara cry from my relentless nitpicking.

After that happened, a friend who loved the Lord said to me, "Daniel, do you realize that the Greek word for 'flesh' is *sarx*? Sarcasm means 'the gnashing of the flesh.' You're relentless with the sarcasm, and Sara is crying!"

I *almost* said something sarcastic back to her! Which helped me believe the whisper of the Spirit in my ear. My friend was right, and the way I was living was wrong.

In this day and age of entitlement and narcissism, humility is in short supply. We like to be in charge and assume our way is the right way, which is why God uses spiritual directors to speak into our lives.

Humility starts in the presence of God. How could it not? God is *God*, and when we are truly in his presence, we cannot help but be humbled. However, humility is *sustained* in the presence of a spiritual director. Not because the director takes the place of God, but because they continually take us back into God's presence. Over and over and over.

Whether we like it or not!

Promise

Are you stuck in a rut? Do you want to get out of it and start following God somewhere glorious and new?

Praise God!

But let me ask you one more thing: Are you humble enough to give someone the power to call you on your garbage?

See, sometimes we like our garbage. Not because it's garbage, usually, but because it's *our* garbage. This is especially risky when our garbage actually looks . . . pretty good! Like if our garbage is raging anger against innocent bystanders, it's hard to pretend it's good to hang on to. But what if our garbage is finally being financially comfortable enough to work on our golf game or to eat out as often as we want to? Or gossiping at work? Or ignoring our spouse to focus on entertainment?

Now before you get all in my face, my point is that whenever we settle, we stop following the daily call of Jesus. We can't afford to settle in *any* kind of lifestyle. Because when we settle, we're creating spiritual inertia. If God wants us to move—or to do whatever—we'd better be ready.

Which leads us to spiritual direction. To a person we allow to speak into our lives and help us stay available to God.

A lot of this might be stuff you already do, by the way, and already *love*. Like having coffee with someone you admire and sharing your heart. Eugene Peterson says it like this: "Spiritual direction takes place when two people agree to give their full attention to what God is doing in one (or both) of their lives and seek to respond in faith."[1]

That doesn't sound too bad, does it?

We say to a spiritual director, "Help me unpack what God is

---

[1] Eugene Peterson, *Working the Angles: The Shape of Pastoral Integrity* (Grand Rapids, MI: Eerdmans, 1989), 150.

doing in my life because I'm not sure I even see it all, let alone understand it. But I want to be ready to respond to God."

Now without further ado, let's read our scripture. It's a longer passage, but it reads easy because it's a letter. Paul wrote this to his friend Timothy:

I thank God, whom I serve, as my ancestors did, with a clear conscience, as night and day I constantly remember you in my prayers. Recalling your tears, I long to see you, so that I may be filled with joy. I am reminded of your sincere faith, which first lived in your grandmother Lois and in your mother Eunice and, I am persuaded, now lives in you also.

For this reason I remind you to fan into flame the gift of God, which is in you through the laying on of my hands. For the Spirit God gave us does not make us timid, but gives us power, love and self-discipline. So do not be ashamed of the testimony about our Lord or of me his prisoner. Rather, join with me in suffering for the gospel, by the power of God. He has saved us and called us to a holy life— not because of anything we have done but because of his own purpose and grace. This grace was given us in Christ Jesus before the beginning of time, but it has now been revealed through the appearing of our Savior, Christ Jesus, who has destroyed death and has brought life and immortality to light through the gospel. And of this gospel I was appointed a herald and an apostle and a teacher. That is why

I am suffering as I am. Yet this is no cause for shame, because I know whom I have believed, and am convinced that he is able to guard what I have entrusted to him until that day.

What you heard from me, keep as the pattern of sound teaching, with faith and love in Christ Jesus. Guard the good deposit that was entrusted to you— guard it with the help of the Holy Spirit who lives in us.[2]

Isn't that great? We should write more letters these days. Pretty sure this wouldn't be as powerful if it was a bunch of texts that Paul sent.

We're not really going to be breaking down individual words in this passage, although that would be awesome. Rather, we're going to look at this like a story. It's the tale of a wise Christian pouring into the life of a growing Christian.

And we're going to pull some broad points out of it. I'll even give them to you now. A spiritual director

- points us to Jesus,
- helps us see ourselves,
- challenges and encourages us, and
- helps us grow more like Jesus in the way we act.

I don't know about you, but I want that stuff! Actually, I *do* know about you. All of us want that stuff, even if we try to

---

[2] 2 Timothy 1:3-14.

tell ourselves we don't. The reason is that we know this is the good life. Not the distracted life or the pampered life or the apathetic life. The *good* life, where we smile at the end of the day because of the ways we saw Jesus at work.

Point toward Jesus

True spiritual direction always focuses on Jesus. It shines a light on Jesus. Center stage, so all eyes are drawn to him.

We need that every day!

We need someone to remind us who Jesus is, what Jesus has done, and what Jesus promises, because that's the only way lasting transformation happens.

Look back to the passage and you'll see something cool: Paul is convinced that Timothy *doesn't need Paul.*

We'd consider Paul to be pretty amazing—for sure in the top half-dozen figures in world history when it comes to Christianity. But Paul knows that Timothy doesn't need more Paul. What Timothy needs is more Jesus.

And Paul says that every time he prays, he's praying for Timothy. Do you have anyone like that? Who prays for you all the time? Who always thinks about how to bring you back again to Jesus?

Paul actually mentions two of those people, beside himself: Timothy's mother and grandmother. Paul is stoked for Timothy because he's the heir of a spiritual inheritance. His family has provided him with an example of godliness that's lived out. And that's another cool feature of a spiritual director. They see *you*, the individual, not some generic Christian. They take the time to learn who you are, where you've come from, who your family is, and so on. Paul's letter is specifically to Timothy.

Jesus spirituality is never "one size fits all." Which isn't a surprise, given that God knows how many hairs are on our heads and loves us before we're even born.

For each individual, God has a unique idea for how his grace and mercy will become flesh. Like with the greatest commandment, we *start* at the same place, but me loving my neighbor is going to look different from you loving your neighbor.

Before we look at how a spiritual director helps us truly see ourselves, let me give you a real-life example of someone who loved me, in all my specific individuality, and made it his priority to point me to Jesus.

If not for John Henry Corcoran, I wouldn't be a pastor, and you wouldn't be reading this book. God used him to change the direction of my life. When I was twenty-three years old, Pastor John Henry took me under his wing. Actually, that's not quite the right picture—it's more like he put me in a headlock! He said to me, "Daniel, I don't want to make you into what *I* want you to be. I want to see you become all that Jesus died and rose again for you to be."

And he worked for years on that vision. Not *his* vision, but the vision of what Daniel Fusco was designed by God to do.

Once We See Jesus, We Can See Ourselves

Seeing Jesus is how we see ourselves.

Here's a quote that has been spreading around lately. It's so memorable that you'll either be like, "Fusco, *thank* you," or else you'll be like, "Dude, I've already journaled that in my Moleskine!" Either way, here it is: "Humility is not thinking less of yourself. Humility is thinking of yourself less."[3]

We're absolutely not going to be talking about our need to rip ourselves to shreds or tear ourselves down all the time. That's not humility. It's not the way of Jesus either. Honesty can be taken too far. Think of the dour-faced believer you know—we all know at least one—who's always looking for the cloud around every silver lining. Even when they have to ignore the plain truth to do so!

Like you tell someone, "This cake you baked is un-freaking-believable!"

And they go, "No, it's not. It's not that good. I can barely crack an egg."

Or you tell someone, "You are so talented!"

And they go, "Don't say that. I suck."

Those are *not* examples of humility, okay? Those are just examples of people acting lame! Humility includes being honest about your strengths and skills as well as about your weaknesses and limitations.

Here's another helpful definition of humility: clearly seeing yourself *and* the context in which you live.

Meaning humility is seeing others clearly, too. And if you can't see everything they see, then you withhold judgment or comment. Say your boss makes a decision you think is just the worst, so you tell your coworker your opinion. Except

---

3 If you *have* heard it, then I'll give you a bonus. Despite what you've been told, C. S. Lewis did *not* say it, even though about a hundred sources say he did. Rick Warren did. So now you can use a snobby voice when this quote comes up next. *"Actually . . ."* (Rick Warren, *The Purpose Driven Life: What on Earth Am I Here For?* [Grand Rapids, MI: Zondervan, 2012], 190–91.)

what you don't know is that your boss made that decision *instead* of a much worse decision.

We do stuff like this all the time. Like one Saturday morning my oldest daughter came downstairs with her siblings trailing behind her. She was the leader.

"Dad, can we get ice-cream sandwiches?"

I'm an anytime-ice-cream kind of guy, so I thought about it for a sec. They asked the right parent, that's for sure. But then I was like, "Wait, it's eight thirty in the morning!"

"But why not?"

"Because . . . it's eight thirty in the morning!"[4]

"So?"

"So . . . um . . . so you need some protein to start your day off right."

"But doesn't milk have protein?"

I don't know where they learned to debate like that. Probably from their mother. (I love you, babe!)

(Before I make my point here, I know you're wondering whether they got the ice-cream sandwiches or not. They did. But not until almost ten o'clock, after they'd had some healthier food.)

The point, though, is that they weren't seeing themselves with biblical humility—which is to say, honesty in light of Jesus. They didn't see that their bodies need vitamins and nutrients to grow and be healthy. All they could see was their immediate desire for sugar!

Now this example doesn't matter one bit in the grand

---

4 Do you ever recycle reasons as a parent? I do. I figure if they were good enough the first time, then they're good enough the fifth time.

scheme of life, which is why I picked it. I don't want to shame my kids here. But don't we do the same thing, except with issues that are far more important than breakfast? Like my kids that morning, we see only what we want to see.

Jesus, though, sees the full context. How could he not? John's Gospel tells us that *nothing exists* unless it was brought into being by Jesus.[5] And Paul tells us that if we are in Jesus, we are new creations.[6]

Keeping our eyes on Jesus is the only way for us to see ourselves honestly and in context.

Challenge and Encourage

Thank goodness for spiritual directors. They direct our focus to Jesus, despite everything distracting us. And they make sure that when we come face-to-face with Jesus, we see ourselves for who we really are.

Once we have that foundation, we can begin to live for God.

Which sounds great—until we discover that it's really hard. Which is exactly why a spiritual director is someone who will challenge us *and* encourage us.

Let me show you a verse that gets at this truth. In 1 John 3:16-18, we read,

> This is how we know what love is: Jesus Christ laid
> down his life for us. And we ought to lay down
> our lives for our brothers and sisters. If anyone has

---

[5] John 1:3.
[6] 2 Corinthians 5:17.

material possessions and sees a brother or sister in need but has no pity on them, how can the love of God be in that person? Dear children, let us not love with words or speech but with actions and in truth.

That's what I mean by challenging and encouraging at the same time.

The Bible is challenging to the extreme. Every day we see someone in need. But how often do we pretend not to or just pass by? Even if it's a situation as simple as me walking toward someone lying on the sidewalk who looks hungry. Half the time my heart goes straight to how *I'm* hungry and how if I help this person, I won't have the cash in my wallet for that burrito I want.

And the Bible links that inability—unwillingness?—to help to a lack of God's love in us.

Yikes. Pretty much makes *challenging* look like the wrong word. More like impossibly depressing.

But that's where the encouragement comes in! Because we remember (or because our spiritual directors remind us) that Jesus saw *us* in need and then did something about it. He came to earth for us. The love of God wasn't just *in* Jesus . . . it overflowed, pouring out into the whole world.

So the switch gets flipped in a single breath. We breathe in, and we're failing again. We breathe out, and we're children of the King of kings, empowered by *his* love and mercy and grace to share love and mercy and grace with those in need. (And to share food, too!)

Remember Pastor John Henry? He knew that when I first

started preaching, I didn't have any business being in a pulpit, and he didn't want things to stay that way.

He'd tell me things that encouraged me, such as "God's given you a gift of teaching, Daniel. He wants to use you in a powerful way."

That felt great! But the reason I could trust him was that he also said, "Man, your gift is *totally* unrefined." And he'd give me books to read and sermons to listen to, and he'd pray with me and tell me when one of my sermons fell flat or was wrong-hearted.

Encouragement and challenge. A spiritual director is willing to say things to us no one else will. Not because they want to tear us down, though, but because they're so convinced that God wants to use us in new ways.

We actually looked at this idea back at the start of the chapter. I mentioned that sometimes our garbage looks pretty un-garbage-like. I tried to sell it softly then, so you'd keep reading! But here's the most provocative way I can say it now: Working your tail off for forty years so that you can retire and relax *is not what God sent Jesus to die and rise again for.*

That's scary! I get it.

Which is exactly why God gives us this word: "For the Spirit God gave us does not make us timid, but gives us power, love and self-discipline."[7]

Challenge and encouragement, right? We can do this! Not by our might and not by our power, but by God's Spirit.

Brothers and sisters, if we're going to be afraid, let's be

---

[7] 2 Timothy 1:7.

afraid of things *that are actually scary*. Trying to live into the plans God has for us, and trying to stay willing and ready to hear God's direction, and being truly honest about who Jesus is and who we are? Yep, scary.

So let's not waste our time being afraid of some weak stuff. Like we're afraid we're being "persecuted" because some coffee chain took the word *Christmas* off its cups.

God doesn't promise us that restaurants will honor him.

But God *does* promise us that his strength is made perfect in our weakness. God *does* promise us that he created us, individually, to do good works and build his Kingdom. God *does* promise us that his love and mercy will be enough for us, and that he will always provide for our needs.

Be challenged.

And be encouraged.

Promote Growth

By now we can see why spiritual direction has to be relational and ongoing. We don't become like Jesus overnight. And unless someone knows us—unless we honestly share our lives with someone—we can fall through the cracks.

You might be thinking, *Fusco, we already do this. It's called church. I go every Sunday, and my pastor is amazing. Can we just move on to the next chapter?*

Not yet—I have to put myself down first, and you don't want to miss that!

Preaching is important. Preaching opens the Word to people. Preaching can be powerful. God uses preaching to build the Kingdom.

But preaching as spiritual mentoring or direction? It stinks.

When we listen to a sermon, we don't hear the actual message. Instead we hear the version of the message we preach to ourselves. Like I say something about Jesus fasting, and you start to wonder if you turned the oven off before leaving for church. Or I say something about God knowing everything we've ever done, and you start to wonder what the score of the football game is.

Plus, we can hear the best, most godly, most challenging, most encouraging sermon in the history of sermons . . . and then leave and never change.

Spiritual directors are the ones who follow up. Who take the Word and *integrate* it into your life, making sure we're walking the talk.

Jesus spirituality is rooted in friendships, not isolation. For every supermonk who achieves some kind of isolated holiness, there are *thousands* of people growing into holiness in the context of relationships.

Here's the thing: Jesus won't be formed in you unless you say yes, over time and in relationship with other believers. Spiritual growth is not about someone downloading everything they know to us. It's not a one-way flow of information. When Paul mentors Timothy, part of the process is sharing his own heart, his own struggles, with Timothy.

A spiritual director says, "You share with me—I'll share right back!"

God is deeply interested in our relationships. Holy

relationships are the mechanisms by which we're reminded of the Good News we already believe and by which we're encouraged to keep going and keep growing. A spiritual director is rarely, if ever, going to tell us a brand-new idea about God. We already know what we need . . . it's just that we need help doing it and being honest about it.

I need to challenge you on something before this section ends. Because some of you are thinking, *Sweet, relationships!* And you're jumping from that word straight to people who *cannot be your spiritual director.*

We may *wish* those holy, directing relationships could be the ones we already have with our besties or our buds. We may want our spouses to be our spiritual directors. But it doesn't work like that.

If you're newly married—or especially if you're *about* to get married—you might not believe me on the spouse front. You probably have these ideas about what your married spiritual life is going to be like. You're going to get up an hour before dawn every morning, praying and fasting, and you won't even own a TV because the two of you will be so busy memorizing Scripture and quizzing each other.

I don't want to burst your bubble too fast here. You'll figure it out. But let's just say that your spouse is not the Holy Spirit in your life. Your spouse will learn there are certain issues they won't go near with a ten-foot pole. Nor should they. Some things are better dealt with in other sorts of relationships. And that's why a spouse can't be a spiritual director: because some things are off-limits.

And on the friend front, what usually happens is that our

friends reinforce all the junk we have in our hearts. Like we tell them how *mad* we are about something, and they're like, "Yeah, you *should* be mad about that!"

Whereas a spiritual director will be like, "How does you getting upset about that restaurant give glory to God?"

Any real spiritual director will focus right in on our blind spots. Spouses, friends, family members . . . they all have ulterior motives when it comes to us. That's not a bad thing, really, but it is a thing that prevents them from being our spiritual directors.

However, our spouses and friends and families will be the ones who see the fruit that spiritual direction can produce in our lives. They'll notice how we're patient or more kind or that we dare new things for the sake of our King.

The direction, though, comes from a real spiritual director—from someone who is willing to join us at the feet of Jesus and help us discover what he's up to.

Created to Be

A spiritual director has one goal for us: to help us see God's heart and become more like Jesus.

This isn't about how old we are. Or how long we've been following Jesus. Or about how successful we are. (Or aren't.)

We all need someone who is making an investment in us.

It's important to realize that *all* of life is infused with God's presence, plans, and purposes. That's exactly what a spiritual director can help us see. Sometimes we start to think that certain parts of our lives matter spiritually, and then we just hit autopilot for the other parts of our lives. But every moment is a chance to become more like Jesus—and to reflect Jesus to our hurting world.

However, not every moment is a chance for us to do whatever we want for God! That's one of the main dangers of our affirmation culture. We're told, "You can do anything you want. You can be anything you want!"

Nope.

Now, it's good to expand our options, for sure. And sinful humans use things that aren't of God to wrongly limit or determine people's futures.[8]

Having said that, we absolutely cannot be *anything* we want. Like me, I want to be an NBA center. Notice I said *want*, present tense. Unfortunately, I've got the Napoleon complex going on. Big on the inside . . . not *quite* so big on the outside. But I want to be the dude who's just clogging up the lane, you know? And every time someone tries to bring the ball into the paint, I just step up and swat the ball away into the fifteenth row. And on offense, I want to be throwing down those alley-oops and just stuffing it in people's faces.

For the New York Knicks. Did I mention that part?

Anyway, I can't do that. Not when I was younger, not now, not ever. I'm like five foot eight on a good day. There aren't even any water boys that short in the NBA, okay? My vertical could barely clear a broomstick. I'm just being honest with you.

So we do ourselves a disservice when we tell one another we can do whatever we want. That nothing is impossible.

---

[8] Like how it used to be that women couldn't be surgeons, to pick one example out of almost infinity.

Spiritual directors help us understand who we've been created to be, remember. Which means that if we're absolutely *terrible* at learning languages and if we can't drink tap water without getting diarrhea, our spiritual directors will make sure we don't sign up to be a missionary in Papua New Guinea.

We absolutely are created to be *someone*. God made you *you*, and me *me*, for a reason. And since it's God's reason, you can count on it being deeply good and redemptive.

We're all in process, together, figuring out how to walk through a broken world with grace, love, truth, mercy, compassion, kindness, and faith. We all need people to help us grow and keep Jesus at the center of our lives.

How do we keep wide-open hearts in this heartbreaking world?

How do we continue to step out in faith when our last step ended up with a black eye or a broken life?

How should we treat our spouses or our kids? How should we approach our jobs or the way we talk about politics?

We do it together. We figure it out together. We figure it out with Jesus at the center.

Oh, and one more thing.

I know this chapter is about you. I know this movement is inward. I know we're talking about how to love ourselves. But everything I said in this chapter about spiritual direction and our need for humility? You're meant to *be* that person for someone else as well. You're meant to pay it forward. God has designed us to have mentors and to be mentors.

If we are in God's Word as often as possible, allowing God's Spirit to speak to us, this will happen.

And we—along with the people we come into contact with—will be changed for the better.

Practice

 A godly spiritual director always

- focuses on God's Kingdom and design,
- loves God's Word,
- cares about *you*,
- listens well, and
- models humility.

 Given those characteristics, who have your greatest "directors" been? What did they teach you?

 What do you need to learn at this point in your life, and who might teach you? Pray about whether you should ask that person, even if it seems uncomfortable.

 Whom can *you* teach?

 Remember, spiritual direction is something all of us are called to. There are simple questions that can get you started and easy actions you can take. Consider the following list.

Hey, what about _____? Are you approaching that the way Jesus would?
I heard you were _____. Is that true?
Where do you see Jesus leading you right now?

Is there anything you're scared to try or do right now?

What verses have you been thinking about lately?

Can we pray with each other? What do you want me to pray about?

NOW WHAT?

Now we roll up our sleeves and get to work.

We're loving God with every fiber of who we are. We understand and love ourselves in light of Jesus. And now God's Spirit sends us out into the world.

We're going to spend all of Movement Three looking at how we love our neighbors, but here's a teaser: It's the same way God loves us.

Loving others has everything to do with the work of God's Spirit. We'll see this all through this movement, especially in chapter 3.3, about community. When God's Spirit shows up, the church goes out into the world.

That's what happened at Pentecost, which you can read about in Acts 2. Jesus had promised his friends that after he left he'd send them a helper. Which initially might sound lame, if not for the fact that the helper is God's Spirit. And that God's Spirit will stay with us forever and teach us all things and remind us of everything Jesus said and did . . . *and* produce in us eternal fruit such as peace and kindness and faithfulness, for our sake and the sake of the world.

With *that* Spirit inside us, how could we *not* go into the world in love?

That's exactly how it's been, all around the world, in every generation, since Pentecost.

God's Spirit inspires and empowers people to build God's Kingdom in the name of Jesus. And remember, that kind of Kingdom building actually comes *naturally* to us—as long as we're linked up with God—because of the needs we've been created with. We long for this stuff!

These needs give us a window into our destiny. We're *supposed* to seek after their fulfillment. And the Spirit of God shows us the way of fulfillment: the Father's love through Jesus' sacrifice. Our need for justice, for self-expression, for relationship, and for compassion . . . those were given to us by our Creator, *for the sake* of our neighbors.

Learning the art of living and loving outward isn't just fulfilling our own needs. It's also learning to transform the world.

Are you ready to look out?

justice / service

Problem

If this book were a banana split, we'd already have eaten the two best flavors of ice cream, plus all the whipped cream and the cherry-in-name-only. Hopefully, though, you'll find this final movement—where we look at the art of living *outward*—is way more satisfying than a melty pile of your third-favorite flavor of ice cream.

Because it's time to make a difference by getting to work. Not on ourselves, but on our broken world. And this has everything to do with the Holy Spirit.

I know I don't need to prove brokenness to you, so I won't. It's all around us. We've all had our hearts broken.

We've all been part of breaking others. That's why all of us long for restoration. For wholeness and fairness. For righteousness to prevail and for evil to be defeated.

The Bible calls that justice, and all of us long for it.

Now, there are certain streams of Christianity where that word gets a bad rap—just as there are certain streams where *justice* almost replaces *Jesus*. We get a lot of different messages about justice.

Fortunately, the Bible is very clear about justice. Seriously! Justice is biblical. God is a just God. God's people are called to act justly.

Every day we get more and more evidence that in our world, things are not the way they could be or should be. We look at something and think, *Wait, that's not fair. That's not right.* Things are slanted or upside down or backward. We don't understand why a person or a group of people are suffering or attacked or marginalized or ignored. All we know is that it doesn't sit well with us.

Why do companies or governments sometimes get away with poisoning citizens and the environment? Why do we trample one another on Black Friday when nearly 750 million people have no access to clean water?[1] Why is it that in our country women and minorities are paid less than men and Caucasians for the same work? Why is it that professional athletes make obscene amounts of money for playing a game and professional teachers make so much less? In our cities there are people who have hundreds of millions

---

[1] "World Water Day: Nearly 750 Million People Still without Adequate Drinking Water," UNICEF, March 20, 2015, https://www.unicef.org/media/media_81329.html.

of dollars, and there are people who get their food out of
Dumpsters and trash cans. Why?

I don't know. I can't answer questions like these for you,
but I can ask them—and I hope you keep asking them too.
Our *job* as the people of God is to ask the questions. What
does a just world look like? What does a fair world look like?
How would Jesus change this?

We start in God's Word. The word *justice* shows up 130
times in the NIV, from Genesis to Revelation. And the concept is all over Scripture. *All* over.[2]

In Micah 6:8 we read a fascinating Q&A:

> And what does the LORD require of you?
> To act justly and to love mercy
> and to walk humbly with your God.

That's the kind of clear (and clearly difficult) requirement
given to us in God's Word regarding justice. Timothy Keller
puts it this way:

> If a person has grasped the meaning of God's
> grace in his heart, he will do justice. If he doesn't
> live justly, then he may say with his lips that he
> is grateful for God's grace, but in his heart he is
> far from him. If he doesn't care about the poor,
> it reveals that at best he doesn't understand the
> grace he has experienced, and at worst he has not

---

[2] If you'd like to read more about it, there are many great resources. To start with, check out Timothy
Keller's *Generous Justice: How God's Grace Makes Us Just* and Ken Wytsma's *Pursuing Justice: The Call to
Live and Die for Bigger Things*.

really encountered the saving mercy of God. Grace should make you just.[3]

Which is why our longing for justice is satisfied with service.

Service is not some sort of spiritual discipline we do every so often or seasonally. It's an entire way of orienting our lives.

See, true Christianity isn't a set of beliefs we hold. Rather, it's a set of beliefs that *necessarily lead us into a new way of living and being.*

Although we'd never say this out loud—probably—we might think we can be Christians but act exactly like our culture. If we *believe* the right ideas . . . well, that's where we stop sometimes.

Does our faith make us stand out? It should! Not necessarily like that guy every town has, who stands on a corner and yells at people, eyes raging, while shaking a Bible and holding a handmade sign. He stands out, but not for the right reasons. The *right* reason to stand out is that we're acting like Jesus in the world.

Our neighbors don't need us yelling at them.

They need us to be on mission, led by God's Spirit. Because we're all longing for justice, just like we're all longing to make a difference in the world.

Promise

Jesus knew he was going to die. Keep that in mind when you read this astounding passage of scripture, which takes place the same night he's arrested.

---

3 Timothy Keller, *Generous Justice: How God's Grace Makes Us Just* (New York: Penguin, 2012), 93–94.

It was just before the Passover Festival. Jesus knew that the hour had come for him to leave this world and go to the Father. Having loved his own who were in the world, he loved them to the end.

The evening meal was in progress, and the devil had already prompted Judas, the son of Simon Iscariot, to betray Jesus. Jesus knew that the Father had put all things under his power, and that he had come from God and was returning to God; so he got up from the meal, took off his outer clothing, and wrapped a towel around his waist. After that, he poured water into a basin and began to wash his disciples' feet, drying them with the towel that was wrapped around him.

He came to Simon Peter, who said to him, "Lord, are you going to wash my feet?"

Jesus replied, "You do not realize now what I am doing, but later you will understand."

"No," said Peter, "you shall never wash my feet."

Jesus answered, "Unless I wash you, you have no part with me."

"Then, Lord," Simon Peter replied, "not just my feet but my hands and my head as well!"

Jesus answered, "Those who have had a bath need only to wash their feet; their whole body is clean. And you are clean, though not every one of you." For he knew who was going to betray him, and that was why he said not every one was clean.

When he had finished washing their feet, he put on his clothes and returned to his place. "Do you understand what I have done for you?" he asked them. "You call me 'Teacher' and 'Lord,' and rightly so, for that is what I am. Now that I, your Lord and Teacher, have washed your feet, you also should wash one another's feet. I have set you an example that you should do as I have done for you. Very truly I tell you, no servant is greater than his master, nor is a messenger greater than the one who sent him. Now that you know these things, you will be blessed if you do them."[4]

Now it's *our* turn to "know these things" and be blessed when we do them. Not for ourselves, either, though we will certainly be blessed. But we are blessed in order to be a blessing. People blessed by God are given an opportunity. The Spirit of God invites the people of God to serve the world at its places of pain, in the name of Jesus, to satisfy our need for justice. We have the power to bring justice to an unjust world.

That happens when we serve.

How do I know? Because that's what Jesus did, and before he died he told his friends that if they did the same thing, they'd do even greater things than he'd done.

(I didn't italicize anything in that last sentence, but I hope you caught the mind-blowing part of it.)

---

4 John 13:1-17.

With that story in mind, let's look deeper at a few aspects of our scripture. We'll see how Jesus washing feet teaches us what service is. We'll connect that with our longing for things in the world to be fair and just. And we'll be challenged by how our desire to make a difference is doomed to failure unless Jesus first makes a difference in us.

Foot Washing

Okay, Jesus is having his last meal with his friends.

Now if I was having my last meal—like if the angel Gabriel showed up and told me I only had one more chance to eat—I wouldn't say, "Oh, I'll just have something simple, because I want to make sure to pray with my friends and wash their feet."

Good thing Jesus isn't like me! (Understatement alert.) Instead, he gets up from the meal, takes a towel and bucket of water, and begins to wash his disciples' feet. To what end? Well, one reason is in this quote from Richard Foster, which I love: "Jesus took a towel and a basin and *redefined greatness*."[5] We'll come back to that idea of greatness later in the chapter.

But Jesus also needed to teach his disciples—and us—that love means action. That service is love with hands and feet.

Jesus loves his friends, obviously. But not just with an idea, like, "Hey, love ya, bros!" He loves with the way he acts. He shapes his life in order to serve them.

Now I'm 99 percent sure you've heard people talk about the whole foot-washing thing. How the disciples had gross

---

5 Richard Foster, *Celebration of Discipline: The Path to Spiritual Growth* (New York: HarperCollins, 1998), 126. Emphasis added.

sandal feet and fungus-y fishermen feet. How the streets and alleys had a variety of junk in them that was worse than dirt. How there were good reasons washing feet was the absolute lowest job you could imagine.

Instead of going into all that, I'm going to tell you a story.

One time, about ten years ago, my grandma Anita and grandpa Anthony were over at our house, hanging out. At one point, Grandma catches my eye and says, real sweetly, "Danny?" And right then I know I'm on the hook for whatever comes next. So I'm hoping it's something good—asking if I want to help her whip up some fresh cannoli—and not something bad. Either way, though, I'm doing it.

"Danny . . . can you help your grandpa with his toenails?"

I said sure right away, of course. And then she follows up with, "Usually I take him to the doctor . . . "

I walk over to the couch, and there's my grandfather, sitting there with his shoe off and one leg stretched out. Now before I describe what I saw, let me say that Grandpa has earned the right to have his feet look however he wants. He's a World War II veteran, and he's lived a long and love-filled life. I am blessed to have him in my life, more than words can express. The guy is amazing.

The nail on his big toe was also amazing, in the same way that projectile vomiting can be amazing.

It wasn't just that the nail was really thick, which it was. Like three nails glued together. And it wasn't just that it was yellow and gnarled, which it was. The main thing that grossed me out was that it was growing up, about a ninety-degree angle away from what it was supposed to be.

"Grandpa," I said, "your feet are *nasty*."

He looked at me and smiled. "My feet are *old*."

No comeback to that! I wished I could have used some kind of circular saw on it. If I had, there would definitely have been sparks and smoke flying off. Instead I made do with a serrated knife from the kitchen. I started sawing and hacking at that thing. I asked Grandpa if it was hurting him, and he was like, "Danny, I can't feel a thing down there. Keep working."

So I did. And when I was done, the toenail was trimmed, Grandma was happy, and Grandpa went back to yelling at the New York Rangers on TV.

That story is what I think about when I think about Jesus washing the disciples' feet. And he didn't get roped into it by his grandma, as I did. He volunteered.

Now, I love my grandpa and would do anything for him. But I didn't love that job. I wouldn't have chosen it. Which is what makes Galatians 5:13 so cool. Paul tells us, "You, my brothers and sisters, were called to be free. But do not use your freedom to indulge the flesh; rather, serve one another humbly in love."

In God the Father and in Jesus—upward, inward—we are set completely free. If Jesus has set us free, we are truly and eternally and irrevocably free.

But to what end? So that we can *choose* to serve one another, humbly in love, as Jesus served us.

That's powerful.

Provocative, too. Because indulging the flesh is pretty much what we'd always rather do. Not even in dramatic or sinful ways. I'm talking about something as simple as choosing to stay home and watch a ball game instead of helping a friend move to a new apartment. Not to mention helping an *enemy*.

On the other hand, using the freedom we've been given by Jesus to serve one another humbly in love . . . that's loving our neighbors. That's the outward movement of the greatest commandment. That's how justice enters the world.

Neighbors

The Bible doesn't tell us to bring justice to the entire world, though. That's God's job. Our job is to bring justice to our neighbors. So . . . who's your neighbor?

Everybody you know. And everybody you might meet. Simple, right?

But like most things of God, simple and *so hard to live up to*.

We even find it difficult to be civil with our *actual* neighbors, whom we often have a ton of stuff in common with, or with our Facebook friends. Never mind being a neighbor to people in our communities who are very different from us or people in other countries who speak other languages. And so on.

At the same time, we *want* to be good neighbors. We want to be the Good Samaritan of the parable, whom Jesus commends.

Here's how we can.

Have you ever heard someone being praised for being realistic about life? That's a compliment when we compare it to the supposed alternative, like being naive or having our heads in the sand (or clouds).

As we live out Jesus spirituality, though, we need to be sure that being realistic about life isn't where we stop. It's a good place to start. Dealing with facts means that we won't romanticize living in poverty, for example—just like we won't romanticize living in a mansion! Both conditions are fruitful ground for sin and discontent, and both conditions call us to find our true identity and worth in Jesus.

Once we have the facts, though, we have to move beyond them into what's *possible*. Even if—maybe especially if—it doesn't seem realistic.

Throughout history, things tend to change when a group of people says, "This is the way life is now, but it could be different. It ought to be different."

When that group is a bunch of people who follow Jesus, things can get really crazy! Just read the book of Acts. The Spirit moved in some extraordinary ways through the early church.

That is the work of the people of God: to look at our neighbors and ask, "How might God want this situation to be transformed?"

If there was ever a time to live outward, that time is now. God's Word doesn't invite us to find some kind of holy huddle and keep our heads down until the end of time. God has given us *responsibility* in the world. Plus—and never forget this—God has given us a Spirit of power!

Let's roll up our sleeves and get to work. I've heard it said that it's impossible to rock the boat when you're busy rowing it. Too many of us think Jesus wants us to rock the boat. He doesn't. Our angst and our snarky posts and our little tribes . . . that stuff gets in the way of Kingdom building. We have neighbors near and far—and new neighbors to meet—all of whom need Jesus.

Right now terrorism seems overwhelming, right? Well, hearts changed by Jesus aren't hearts that blow up other people. (Before you object, yes—I *am* saying what you think I'm saying.)

Are the schools terrible where you live? What if everyone at your church met with one kid, once a week, to help with homework and life?

Are you upset by how many homeless people live in your town? What if you got to know them, one at a time? Isn't that what Jesus did when he was on earth?

Grab an oar. Start rowing.

This is the Spirit-filled life. This is how the people of God live. This is the church. We see it in Acts 1:8. Jesus is just about to leave his friends for the last time. And these are his last words: "But you will receive power when the Holy Spirit comes on you; and you will be my witnesses in Jerusalem, and in all Judea and Samaria, and to the ends of the earth."

Friends, we can *do* this.

On our own? No chance.

With God's Spirit? The devil doesn't stand a chance of stopping us!

Unless . . . well, let's talk about that in our next section.

Jesus Has to Serve Us Before We Can Serve Others

We're good at starting to serve . . . then stopping. Or getting sidetracked. The problem is illustrated in verses 6 to 11 of John 13. Peter sees Jesus stepping up with the towel and basin, and he's like, "Jesus . . . seriously?"

Jesus tells Peter something familiar. "You don't understand this now, but you will."

Then Peter goes full Peter. I imagine him scooting his feet back out of the way. He's like, "I don't totally get everything that's happening right now, but I know one thing: You are *not* washing my feet. Period."

(Such drama. Remember, a few weeks after the foot washing, when the disciples are fishing and see the resurrected Jesus on the beach, Peter is the one who can't wait for the boat to land. He leaps into the water and swims to shore in order to be with Jesus faster.)

Jesus answers Peter by flipping the script.

Peter—the guy who often gets it right and gets it wrong simultaneously—realizes the rabbi running the show should *not* be the one with ganky fishermen toes between his fingers. Which is true. Except Jesus is no longer talking about literal human feet. Or at least he's not *only* talking about feet.

One of the problems the disciples had was getting hyperfocused on the present and forgetting the bigger picture. Sound familiar? Nah, it doesn't to me either. I always see the bigger picture! (Ahem.)

But Jesus is helping them see, in the actual act of a footwashing service, that something bigger is happening.

Jesus is talking about washing the disciples—and us—in the finished work of the Cross. Jesus says that if he doesn't wash our feet first, we can't wash other people's feet. If he doesn't work in *us*, we can't bring justice and love into the world in his name.

Being people of grace and mercy, we should cut Peter some slack. I doubt that any of us, had we been having that meal with Jesus, would have done any better. Keep in mind, Peter suffered from a serious case of foot-in-mouth syndrome, so his behavior wasn't entirely his fault. We should also remember that God *chose* Peter, on purpose. To be his friend and ministry companion. And also, against all odds, to be a key figure in building his Kingdom and spreading the church across the entire world. That should give any of us train wrecks—I'm raising my hand here—hope.

Friends, the only time the devil can defeat us and stop our service is when we don't allow Jesus to serve us first. There's a necessary order to how this works. A process. Jesus serves us, demonstrating how true love acts, and only then can we serve others. Trying to clean others while we're still dirty will never work—and the only way we can get clean is when Jesus cleans us.

I've got a great story about this. My son is such a fun dude. He has a big personality. He is a total guy, and he showers the way I think all boys shower, which is to let water run over him. No soap, no washing, no scrubbing . . . just water. So it accomplishes exactly nothing. Which would be fine if he didn't stink. He'll take the longest showers and come out to the couch and sit down, and we'll start sniffing. It can be nasty sometimes because he gets into all sorts of junk when he plays outdoors. Where we live, in the beautiful Pacific Northwest, standing water and mud and scummy moss are like sand and cactus in Arizona, okay?

So usually when he's done showering, we'll check in about the soap thing. One time my bride asked, real nicely, "Did you use soap?"

He told us he definitely used soap.

My wife was not convinced, so she took one for the team and performed the sniff test, and you could instantly tell she regretted it. He still stank something awful. So she told him to get his butt back upstairs and use soap.

It seemed like it wasn't thirty seconds later that he came bounding back down. My wife did her eyebrow thing—which I was loving since it was directed at a Fusco male who wasn't me—and walked over to him. "There ain't *no way* you got clean that fast."

Sniff test, take two. She looked at him, eyes narrowed. He looked at her, eyes dancing, with the smile of a little angel.

Then she said, "Wow. I was wrong. You smell . . . pretty good actually!"

He grinned. She sat back on the couch.

Except it wasn't long before he started itching, and squirming, and complaining.

So my wife asked him what was wrong.

"I dunno, but I *itch*! I think maybe it's from the air freshener I sprayed all over myself."

Believe me, he was not happy when we made him shower right then, with soap. There was some kind of chemical reaction between the soap and the air freshener, and let's just say that he won't try the Febreze trick again, at least until he gets to college.

So here's the thing: That story describes all of us. Every time we try to make ourselves clean with anything other than Jesus, we're just spraying ourselves with air freshener.

God knows we need to be clean, though. Which is why he sent Jesus. Jesus cleanses us by his death and resurrection. He serves us by living the life we should live, but fail to, and by dying the death we deserve on our behalf. By sheer grace, God applies Jesus' perfection to us. And we all say, "Hallelujah!"

Jesus washed his disciples' feet to show them what he could do to their hearts. To *our* hearts. Having our hearts washed by Jesus is the only way we'll be able to wash anyone else. Hearts cleaned by Jesus are God's plan for transforming the world.

Notice the end of the interaction between Peter and Jesus.

Peter, bless him, *starts* to catch on . . . but he doesn't quite get all the way. He decides to go all-in. "Fine, Jesus—but if you're going to wash my feet, wash my hands and head, too!"

Except he's still thinking about actual water, remember, and not what Jesus is going to do to clean our hearts.

We are already clean. What did Jesus say on the cross? It is finished! *But we keep living as if we're unclean.* We keep trying to spray on some air freshener and then do a few "good deeds" in the world, whenever we're not too busy. We'll be "good people" who try to "help others."

That's small potatoes. Little stuff. And we *still* can't sustain it on our own.

That's not what Jesus died for. That's not the reason Jesus

told his disciples they'd be given a Spirit of power or the reason he promised them they'd do even greater things than he'd done.

We hunger for justice because we know life isn't fair. But we chase the wrong stuff. We change our Facebook status. We send around a good link. We act grumpy. We complain while we listen to the news. We update our profile pictures with special colors that mean something.

Baloney.

You're like, "Fusco, give me a break—it's small, but at least I'm doing *something*, right?"

Wrong.

Jesus didn't create you and serve you and clean you, forever, from the inside out, just so that you could be satisfied with pocket change.

The main reason people don't follow Jesus is because they don't see the people of Jesus serving the way Jesus served. They see us worried about haircuts and dancing instead of healing sick people and creating meaningful jobs. Empowered by God's Spirit, let's dare to start serving. We'll make mistakes, yes, but we'll be asking questions along the way—and we'll be avoiding the worse mistake of keeping to ourselves, in isolation. I believe with all my heart that the reason the world isn't more livable and just is that God's people *go* to church instead of *being* the church.

Remember how I said we'd come back to the idea of greatness? Matthew 20:26-28 says, "Whoever wants to become great among you must be your servant, and whoever wants to be first must be your slave—just as the Son of Man did not come to be served, but to serve, and to give his life as a ransom for many."

If you want to be great, be a servant. That's the way of Jesus. Jesus didn't come to be served, but to serve others. It fits right in with the movement of the greatest commandment. Upward, inward, outward. We start with God's creative and proactive love. Then we see ourselves rightly—not as superheroes, but as people changed by Jesus.

And then, empowered by the Spirit, we go into the world, in the name of Jesus. Let's be motivated by what the Lord requires: that we do justly, love mercy, and walk humbly with God.

And let's be inspired, because when we do those things, we find that a life of service is the life we've been longing for.

Practice

🔁 Start close to home. We have a tendency to go straight from *not* serving to deciding we need to start a ministry in China. But in Acts 1:8, Jesus shows us a natural progression from local to global. We might end up serving globally, but typically we should start close to home.

🔁 So if you're married, serve your spouse. If you're in assisted living, serve those around you. Serve your coworkers. If you're living above the garage, serve your parents. If you're a parent, serve your kids. If you're a student, serve your teachers. If you're a boss, serve your employees.

🔁 Do you feel called to serve in a particular area, yet you feel a sense of apathy or even resentment? Read

1 Corinthians 13. Pray for a heart that is filled, above all, with the love of Jesus. Begrudging service isn't service . . . it's us trying to do "good works" for the wrong reasons.

↗ Use your stuff to serve others. Everything we have in our lives is a gift from God. (Yep, even *that* thing, and that *other* thing.) God's grace loves to redeem, to make beauty out of ugly things. Consider whether the things you've done, or the things that have been done to you, might be opportunities to serve in the name of Jesus, with the goal of transforming hearts.

↗ Take an inventory of your current life. Are you working for justice in the world? How and where? What could you be doing differently? Would other people describe you as a servant? Do you let Jesus serve you? What does the service of Jesus teach you about how you could serve others?

3.2

self-expression / creativity

Problem

Think about the times in your life when you've felt like nobody sees you. That nobody knows you as *you*.

Sure, you may still have friendly neighbors or coworkers. You may still be part of a rec-league basketball team or a book club. But you feel as if, in the eyes of everyone else, you could be *anyone*. You could be replaced. You're generic, not unique.

That's the opposite of how we're meant to feel.

It's not just that we long for self-expression, for uniqueness—we were *created* for that by a creative God.

Even if we don't think of ourselves as expressive people,

we're constantly expressing and broadcasting ourselves to others. The clothes we wear, how we wear them, and which occasions we wear them on. Music, hair, vehicles, hobbies, neighborhoods, food, sports teams, social networking, schools . . . the list of how we project our unique selves goes on and on.

The reason we can still feel as if no one sees us, or that we aren't truly who we are meant to be, is that stuff like musical taste and clothing choices aren't sufficient ways to express ourselves. (Yes, I'm hearing '80s Madonna in my head right now, and I hope you are too!)

The only thing that will truly satisfy our need for creative self-expression is a lifestyle, not a new haircut or our team winning a championship. We limit ourselves to those narrow alleys of creativity as we age. We get used to the idea of being uncreative in nearly everything we do.

But we don't start out that way.

On any given Sunday there are more than a hundred second graders in classrooms at the church I pastor. Second graders are a generally awesome bunch. They occupy a kind of sweet spot between younger and older kids. As I write this, my daughter Maranatha is a second grader. Much younger and you're dealing with wet pants and tantrums, plus lots of drool. Much older, though, and you start to get stinky feet (and armpits), plus eye rolling.

One of the things that makes second graders awesome is that they *know* they're awesome—which makes them happy. Like they'll tell you they are the best puppy trainer in the universe or that they are the best at math. They're not bragging so much as they are delighting in the truth.

I bring up second graders and their general awesomeness because of our topic in this chapter: art and creativity.

If you go into a room full of seven- and eight-year-olds and ask, "How many of you will be professional athletes?" you'll get a bunch of raised hands. Same thing if you ask about becoming president or living on Mars. Those numbers are completely out of step with reality, obviously. I'd bet good money that none of those second graders would end up doing those things. A few might, of course, but it's still a safe bet.

But that's not the only thing they'll raise their hands for. If you ask them, "How many of you are artists?" you'll see nearly every hand in the room shoot up.

Contrast that with a room full of adults. How many of us will raise our hands—5 percent? One?

I don't bring this up to point out how silly second graders are. The opposite, really. Their attitude about art and creativity has a lot to teach us. They know more than we do! They naturally express their unique creativity in everything they do, from math to writing to conversations to forest exploration.

When Jesus said, "Truly I tell you, unless you change and become like little children, you will never enter the kingdom of heaven,"[1] I think part of what he was talking about is a child's innate sense of creativity.

As we age, we lose our fearlessness. We become less concerned with expressing ourselves than with managing how others see us.

---

[1] Matthew 18:3.

And not for no reason! Expression, at least as we age, involves risk. Over time we learn that some expressions earn us applause or money or approval, while others earn us ridicule or fear or rejection. So the spark of creativity we had inside us as kids, the one that set every idea on fire with possibility, fades to embers. And in some of us—most of us, maybe—it's gone out completely.

Friends, that is not what God intends.

An infinitely creative God created us. And God continues to be creative *in* us, so that we can be creative—in his name—for the sake of the world.

Our call to express ourselves through a lifestyle of creativity is like someone turning on every light in a house at sunset. You've walked or driven past houses that are all lit up, right? What's cool about them is that we can't help but stare! There's something attractive and compelling about a glowing house in a dark neighborhood. (The Bible uses a similar image, by the way, but I'll let you find those examples on your own if you're curious.)

When we give up on living lives of creative expression, it's like we're turning out the lights.

Now if you're paying attention, you're scratching your head. Upward, inward, outward is our theme, and here we are in Movement Three, looking at how to live outward. We just finished a chapter about satisfying our need for justice with service. We're rolling up our sleeves and getting to work in our families and communities, renewed and empowered by the Spirit of God. So why the heck am I talking about creativity—doesn't that belong in our inward discussion?

Nope. (And thanks for that perfect segue, imaginary reader who's paying attention!)

We're not talking about some lonely, isolated, creative genius brooding off in a cabin somewhere. We're talking about real, everyday life. See, creativity and self-expression, which are part of how God designed us to live, *are about better loving God and loving our neighbors.*

Creativity begins inside, but it's not meant to stay there. Creativity is a blessing from God, through us, for the world. And it breaks my heart to write this, but in the fifteen-plus years I've been part of various Christian churches in America, I have never once heard someone preach that truth.[2]

Here's what I'm going to show you in this chapter: You can rediscover the artist that God created you to be.

Think about that. We're not talking about *if* you're an artist or about *if* God designed you to be creative. Those things are already true, for all of us. Instead, we're going to look at the how and the why. And we're going to do more than satisfy our longing for creativity and self-expression.

We're going to join God's Spirit in transforming everything!

Promise

A quick definition before we read our scripture.

Remember how last chapter I said justice is actually easy to define? It's basic fairness and wholeness and rightness, grounded in who God is and who we are. We should not

---

[2] I know some churches do. But more need to. And more often.

pull out our hair trying to define and redefine and argue a concept that is really meant to be understood by *living* it.

Creativity is much the same. There are literally entire books that try to define creativity. I'll do it in one *sentence*: *Creativity is when we tap into who God created us to be in order to make something new and beneficial for the sake of the world.*

It's important not to think that creativity and self-expression describe only fine art. Creativity can mean painting a portrait or painting a house. It applies to creating a song or creating a spreadsheet. As we'll see in our scripture in just a second, all of us are called to be creative and all of us are called to do good works. But clearly not all of us are called to be professional artists. That *must* mean that God has designed ways for us to be creative in our jobs.

Okay, let's look at God's Word. We've been digging into some longer sections in the last few chapters. I'm going to cut you some slack in this chapter, as long as you promise to consider yourself as a creative artist, okay?

Here it is—Ephesians 2:8-10:

> For it is by grace you have been saved, through faith—
> and this is not from yourselves, it is the gift of God—
> not by works, so that no one can boast. For we are
> God's handiwork, created in Christ Jesus to do good
> works, which God prepared in advance for us to do.

I love these verses. Partly for their unexpected connection to creativity, and partly because we've got the whole story of Scripture here in fifty-four words!

Let's start with God being a creative God. That's not mind-blowing to most of us because we believe God created *everything*. Which *is* mind-blowing, actually, but we're so used to the idea that it seems run-of-the-mill.

However, we aren't as comfortable thinking about God's creativity being demonstrated in us, right now. We think that sure, it applies to people in general, maybe. Or specific people who are awesome, maybe.

But me? You?

Yet Ephesians says we are God's handiwork, created in Christ Jesus. That word *handiwork* is incredible. Some translations use *workmanship* or *masterpiece* or *creation*. In Greek it's the word *poēma*. That's where we get our English word *poem*. So Paul is saying that we are God's *poem*. Which is stunning.

I'm not a poet, but I love reading good poems. Poetry has this way of cutting right to the heart of something, doesn't it? Like you've seen a million trees before, but suddenly a poem about a certain tree gives you eyes to truly see it for the first time. A love poem can change the course of a life.[3] Poems are expansive and unique and specific and memorable.

That's who you are. You, the person reading this, are God's poem. God's glorious work of art.

I like this lyric: *You make everything glorious / And I am Yours / What does that make me?*[4] Such a great rhetorical question! We don't usually think like that, but it's true. God is a master artist, and he doesn't make junk.

---

3 True story: My writing partner got his wife to start dating him after he wrote her a love sonnet. I believe the poetic term for that is *wooing*!

4 David Crowder Band, "Everything Glorious," *Remedy* (sixsteps, 2007).

But We're Still in Process

Okay, but don't get a big head about it! It's by *grace* we've been saved. So don't go around saying, "Oh, yeah, I'm totally God's *Mona Lisa*. I'm God's *Moonlight Sonata*." Because we aren't just God's art . . . we're unfinished art. Second Corinthians 3:18 tells us that God's Spirit is transforming us into the image of God. It's still happening![5]

Sometimes Christians will say, "God's not finished with me yet." Usually we bring that up when we screw up. And that's true. But it's also true that God's not finished with the *good* stuff in us either. God's creativity created the world and everyone in it, just like God's creativity is—present tense, *is*—re-creating and refashioning us, day by day.

Look back over the last hour, the last week, the last year. Your whole life.

That's God's canvas—including the pain.

I'm not being flippant here when I say "your whole life." I'm acquainted with how life can slap us around. How it can drip poison into our veins, year after aching year.

But if the Bible is right about us being God's art, pain is to be expected. Paintings have sketches and false starts and errors beneath the final layer. Songs have discarded sections and terrible first versions. In the last chapter we talked about using our "stuff" to serve others. The places where we've been hurt or broken are the places where God shows us how to be truly transformational servants.

God doesn't promise us that bad things won't happen. If a

---

[5] If you want to think more about this idea, via a great work of art, check out C. S. Lewis's *The Great Divorce*.

preacher tells you that, you can officially stop listening. God doesn't promise we won't be hurt. God doesn't promise we'll be rich or healthy or successful.

Know what God does promise? That we'll have trouble in this world—and that we can take heart and be courageous because God's grace and power are sufficient.

When we try to find a savior other than God—something to keep us from ever being hurt or suffering pain—there is always a moment when our so-called savior fails us.

This is especially tempting for certain types of creative artists.

I know because I tried it. Before I met Jesus—but after I had become a solid bass player—I was a professional musician.

After Jesus saved me, I was still struggling with something related to creativity. I was playing gigs all the time, and I was finding my identity in my performances. If it seemed I'd connected with the audience and everyone responded well to how I played, I would feel great about myself. I'd be elated all night and into the next day. But if I got a lousy response from the audience or didn't live up to the vision I had for my own performance, I'd be devastated.

If you're looking to art to be your savior, you're in for a bumpy ride. Art isn't a savior. And it can be a brutal taskmaster.

But *you* are God's art, and God is the only one who can truly save. God is the only one who can take the pain in your life, and the failure in your life, and redeem it . . . not just for your sake, but to transform others as well.

See, we think failure is antithetical to creativity, but really it's the vehicle. Let's go to God's Word. Think of the failures in the pages of Scripture that turned out to be part of God's creative plan. Adam and Eve. Moses. Jacob. David. Paul.

Jesus being put to death. Literally everyone thought that meant the whole thing had failed.

Here's a quick story from music history. The great Charlie Parker, who is one of the great pioneers of jazz, goes to a jam session as a young man. He stands up with his saxophone, and . . . it does not go well. The other musicians are shaking their heads like, "Man, this kid doesn't have it. This isn't working."

Charlie keeps soloing a bit longer, when all of a sudden, there's this big *crash*. The drummer has taken one of the cymbals off the stand and tossed it on the ground—that's how much he didn't like Charlie's solo!

That incident, that failure, became the fuel that propelled Charlie Parker forward. He practiced and performed and practiced and performed, and in time he created an entire genre of jazz called bebop.

We could look at athletes who go undrafted and still become huge successes. We could look at a painter like Van Gogh who scarcely sold any paintings in his lifetime. Or Steve Jobs getting ousted from Apple, then going on to start Pixar, *then* coming back to Apple and setting it on a path to become one of the most successful companies in the world.[6]

We are God's poems, God's works of art—but we're unfinished.

---

[6] "Steve Jobs: A Timeline: CNET Remembers the Key Milestones in Apple Co-Founder Steve Jobs' Life," CNET, October 5, 2011, https://www.cnet.com/news/steve-jobs-a-timeline/.

And thank God for that!

Because the more space there is in us for God to work his creativity, the better.

Saved by Grace, into Works

Our scripture is so short we can read it again.

> For it is by grace you have been saved, through faith—
> and this is not from yourselves, it is the gift of God—
> not by works, so that no one can boast. For we are
> God's handiwork, created in Christ Jesus to do good
> works, which God prepared in advance for us to do.

Now I say this a ton, because it's so important and so misunderstood. We aren't saved *by* works, but we are saved *into* works.

On the one hand, it's tempting to think that doing good things—godly things—is what saves us. It isn't. Our verse is very clear that it is by *grace* we have been saved—by faith, *not* by works. It even tells us why: so that we can't boast about saving ourselves. The saving is 100 percent in God's hands.

On the other hand, it's tempting to stop with the grace part. Christianity rightly gets a bad rap for talking about salvation as if it's a one-time event. As if God gives us a ticket to heaven, we file it in a drawer somewhere, and then we live our lives however we want.

The Bible gives us the best image for how salvation and works function, in both the Old and the New Testaments: fruit.

Picture a peach tree. We don't call it a peach tree only *after* it bears a crop of peaches. It's a peach tree when it's first planted in the ground, a knee-high sapling. At the same time, producing peaches is what that tree *does*. It's not some optional thing. Imagine if you had a peach tree in your yard that seemed healthy and vibrant but never produced fruit. If a friend asked, "Is that a peach tree?" you'd probably say something like "Well, it's a peach tree in *theory*, but . . . "

See how that works?

Another way to say it would be that we don't practice good works to *be* saved, but rather because we *are* saved.

It's the same with art and creativity. We're not saved by creativity, but we're saved into it.

Think back to those second graders we talked about. Or better yet, to yourself when you were small and the world seemed full of magic and mystery and possibility. You could try anything, do anything, be anything.

You could express yourself with creative freedom.

What about now? What does culture tell us to be concerned with? Making money, paying bills, being responsible. Creativity is nice work if you can get it. But most of us can't. Most of us should just give up on discovering who God created us to be.

Sound familiar?

Now think about what God tells us to be concerned with: remembering that we are God's art, created specifically to do good works that God planned out for us before we were even conscious.

Do you think there might ever be, I don't know, the tiniest bit of conflict between those two spheres of concern?

Prepared in advance for us to do . . . that's an invitation to fulfill our destiny. When you were still a twinkle in your parent's eyes, God was already preparing certain things for you do to. That's incredible. That's inspirational. Especially because we're not robots. If God had prepared things for us to do and then created us in a way that we *automatically* did them, what would be the point?

But since we're free, that means God wants us—you and me, specifically—to use our creative gifts and unique self-expression to change the world.

That's what we have to ask God about. We need to be curious about how God has designed us to live outward. I'm not saying we should all stop paying our bills and start acting like "artists." I'm saying we need to understand that God is calling us to live creatively in *everything* we do.

> *God, I've got my job, and I'm trying to take care of business there, but is there anything different I should be doing? And how does that relate to the good works you've prepared for me? How can I make space for you to work in me, so I can work in the lives of others? How can I bring your grace and creativity to my current life? How can I express myself through you?*

When we're ready to start praying like that, God is ready to work in and through us, with unmatched creativity.

Start Small

A long journey starts with a single step.

Super cliché—but true! Mother Teresa said that if you want to feed one hundred people, start by feeding one. It only takes a spark to get a fire going. (I could go on . . . and on and on.)

But I bring up this idea because it's so important for our calling to be creative. I think the biggest barrier to doing something new is fear. We don't know if we'll succeed. We don't know what will happen in a year, or ten. We don't know what other people will think. To protect ourselves, we want to have everything mapped out and planned before we start.

Unfortunately, that isn't how creative expression works. It's not how we accomplish the good works God has prepared for us. We need to be second graders again and just *go for it*.

Take Jean Vanier. Back in 1964, this young French priest had his heart broken. He saw how people with intellectual and physical disabilities were hidden out of sight, in asylums. He knew there had to be a better, more loving way to treat them. He didn't know what to do, exactly, but he didn't let that stop him. He got creative. (See what I did there?)

With help from friends and family, he bought a small house and named it L'Arche (The Ark). He invited two people with disabilities to live there, in safety and with dignity.

Today, only fifty-plus years later, there are about 150 L'Arche communities around the world, serving thousands and thousands of people.[7]

---

[7] L'Arche International, https://www.larcheusa.org/who-we-are/larche-international-2/.

That creative expression of God's love began with one person who was passionate about something. Vanier couldn't predict the future or guarantee success. He just knew that what was right in front of him was unacceptable. He saw how things were, and he wanted them to be different.

What creative works are you going to unleash on the world?

What are you going to do when you fail?

Every area of life needs the people of God to be creative artists in the way they pursue good works in the name of Jesus.

We need Christians who bake bread in the name of Jesus and win awards for it.

We need Christians who play guitars and trade stocks and drill wells and fly airplanes and make laws and raise kids and assemble furniture and dance and write code and clean offices and design houses and throw baseballs.

All in the name of Jesus. All in creative response to our creative God.

All for the sake of the world.

Jesus wants to work in you so that you can work in the world. Which means you need to be unique in Christ.

It's easy to read that and skip right past it. So let's break that down.

You.

This part's easy. I'm talking to you, the person reading this book. Don't think about what someone else should do. Don't apply this to your kid or spouse or boss or enemy. God's speaking to you right now.

Need.

This part's simple but not easy. God created you to do good works. He didn't make some of us workers and others something else. Scripture tells us that faith without works is dead. And that trees that don't bear fruit will be cut down. And that God will separate the righteous from the unrighteous based on their actions toward the vulnerable and the needy. And that if we don't actually help our brothers and sisters in need, the love of God is not in us.

So yeah . . . you *need* to do this.

To be unique.

We usually think of being unique as something to chase or admire, right? Like we see that guy or gal with the sick style, and we think, *I wish I were as unique as they are.*

Sometimes, though, being unique means being willing to give up on a desire. If I truly want to be unique in Christ, I can't be a singer. My singing voice disturbs mating cats, okay? I mean, I *would* be unique if I became a singer, but it would not help the world in the name of Jesus.

But I can be a creative preacher. I can express who God made me to be with my bass.

You need to be uniquely who God made you to be. Unique in Jesus, not unique in the eyes of the world. At the end of the day, your creative expression exists to draw others to Jesus, not to yourself. Which, in a wonderful biblical paradox, will make you incredibly and creatively unique.

In Christ.

We don't want to miss this—it's so important. Too much creativity happens outside of Jesus. It isn't for God's glory or the blessing of humanity. It's designed to celebrate the kingdom of self. And it misses all that is truly and intrinsically beautiful about creativity's intended *end.*

God saves us. We are God's masterpiece. And our creativity was prepared for us by the Lord. So biblical creativity is born in Christ!

Who are *you* in Christ? And what is Jesus up to? How can you join in God's creative act as a partner? How can you see God's masterpiece come into existence by your availability and involvement?

You aren't too old to take a risk. It may feel that way, but you aren't.

Like I wrote this book before my *first* book came out. Which was a risk. But even writing one book is a risk.

When you're an adult, anyway. My kids, though, write books all the time. They staple a whole bunch of papers together and trim the edges with those weird scissors that have patterns in them, and they add words and art and stickers and sometimes snot if they're in an artistic mood when they have a cold, and *voila!*—they have a book.

And they know it's good, and they don't care what anyone else thinks about it.

Actually that's not quite true. They don't care what anyone thinks about it *other than my wife and me.*

We always love it.

That's how we need to think about ourselves and our heavenly Father. God is rooting for us, empowering us, transforming us, gifting us, all because long ago he planned out ways for us to change the world on his behalf.

God wants us to turn on all the lights in our houses.

Right now, do you have only a lamp or two shining? Flip every single switch until your life absolutely shines with your unique, God-given creativity. Whatever you do, whatever age you are, whatever your family shape is, you're meant to shine.

And the world can't wait to see what you and Jesus come up with.

In fact, the world *needs* to see it.

Practice

⟳ Do you have passions in your life that you feel you can't express? What are they? Perhaps God is inviting you to rekindle those passions.

⟳ Teach yourself to appreciate creative things other people do for the sake of God's Kingdom. Ask yourself whether things you think of as uncreative—such as real estate or tutoring or debugging software—might actually be expressions of God's creative goodness.

⟳ Do you believe that God has made you unique for a reason? If not, why not? Ask God to help you see his creative plans in your uniqueness.

3.3

↑ ↙ ↗

relationship / community

Problem

Being human means having relationships.[1]

Mostly that's a good thing. The catalog of benefits we get from relationships is enormous. We tend to be more content when we're with other people. Close friendships are one of the only things that can make us *actually* happier. (Sorry, money.) Relationships can help keep us happier and help us heal faster.

This starts at birth. We've all heard those horror stories about orphaned babies in some faraway country who

---

[1] In other news, water is wet and beans give me gas.

are raised with virtually no human contact. No hugs, no cuddling, no soft voices, no tickling. Tragically, those kids develop abnormally because of the lack of relationship, and they'll suffer for it the rest of their lives.

Even loving relationships, though, can be the scene for some of the deepest human suffering. Unfortunately, everyone has their own stories and wounds from relationships.

I don't want to be a total downer here, but my bride, Lynn, and I both lost our mothers to cancer when were in our early twenties. It broke our hearts. For the two of us, our moms were the center of our lives. We were never able to meet each other's mom either. There isn't a day that goes by that we don't talk about how much our moms would love our crazy kids. And there isn't a day that goes by that we don't feel the heaviness of that loss.

A whole different kind of hard is the loss of people who *choose* to walk out of our lives. It's one thing for someone to die. But it's quite another when someone leaves you because they just don't want to be there anymore.

As a child, I had an uncle whom I was particularly close to. He was a good bowler, and he decided I was his good luck charm, so he'd often take me to the bowling alley. When he'd take his turn, I would turn my ball cap around to help him out—and it worked! And he knew I loved baseball and collecting baseball cards. I was shocked when for my twelfth birthday he presented me with an almost mint-condition 1967 Topps Carl Yastrzemski card.[2]

---

[2] Although I am a die-hard New York sports fan, and thus I always root against the Boston sports teams, the fact that Yaz was a Red Sox didn't bother me at all. He won the Triple Crown in 1967. What a sweet gift and a serious addition to my collection!

So imagine my dismay a few years later when he just . . . left.

He didn't just leave me, either. He left everyone. The entire family. The uncle who I invited to my birthday party every year—not just the family party but the party with all the little dudes—because he was so much fun, just walked out. To be honest with you, I still haven't seen him.

Relationships can be brutal.

Yet all of us need relationships. Always.

I'm not saying we're all extroverts or that we always need to be around other people. There's a whole spectrum of how much we enjoy being with others. Me, I'm somewhere in the middle. I love crowds and conversations and meeting new people, but I also need to chill on the couch with my bass or a book. I'm an omnivert. You might get antsy whenever you're alone, or you may get nervous whenever you leave the house. But all of us are part of a network of actual and potential relationships. Not only because we choose to be, or are forced to be, but also because that's just how we're wired as humans.

The reason is because God is wired this way too! (To be honest, I'm not sure "wired" applies to God, but you know what I mean. It might be better to say God *is* this way.) God is relational, both within the Trinity of Father-Son-Spirit and in relationship to humanity. We see this in the very first chapter of the Bible, and it stretches from there, connecting every important dot until eternity. All of creation is an outgrowth of God's relational nature, just as all of eternity will be.

Which means that each one of us is created for relationship and community as well.

So relationship comes naturally to us. And it's a great start to the art of living. But it's just that: a start.

Relationships aren't the end goal. God hasn't designed us to keep looking and looking until we find the perfect relationship, and then to chill because no relationship is perfect. Rather, God has designed our need for relationship to point us toward community.

And not just any community, but the family of God.

A community of people rooted in God's Word, simply responding to Jesus and empowered by the Spirit, is the *only* community that will truly satisfy our need for relationship—for as long as we're alive. That's because it's the only community that provides the relationships we crave *and* redeems the inevitable pain of those relationships.

That's the art of living upward, inward, outward. And we're meant to live it together.

At this point in Movement Three, we've learned that living outward takes us to the hurting places of the world, as creative expressions of the way God created us, in the name of Jesus. One way to think of community is that it's the foundation we need for that outward movement. It reminds me of a game we used to play at the pool club in New Jersey. The goal was to arrow underwater, all the way across the pool, without kicking. I bet you've played the same game, and if you have, you know the secret is in the push-off. If you get both feet planted firmly against the wall of the pool and flex your knees all the way, you can generate a *ton* of power. But if you're on only one foot or you slip on a bit of tile or that underwater light, you're going to pop up in the middle of the pool to a chorus of laughter from your friends.

Let's get out in the world. Let's make a difference. But let's make sure we're doing it the right way: by first being part of the family of God.

Promise

We're going to start right in with our scripture. This comes from the second chapter of Acts, which is the first book of the New Testament after the Gospels. Basically, it's a record of the consequences of Jesus' perfect life, sacrificial death, and resurrection. It answers the question, *How did the world change after Jesus?*

These verses describe the early church. This first group of Christians—"little Christs"—were living in Jerusalem. And here's a snapshot of their lives:

> They devoted themselves to the apostles' teaching and to fellowship, to the breaking of bread and to prayer. Everyone was filled with awe at the many wonders and signs performed by the apostles. All the believers were together and had everything in common. They sold property and possessions to give to anyone who had need. Every day they continued to meet together in the temple courts. They broke bread in their homes and ate together with glad and sincere hearts, praising God and enjoying the

favor of all the people. And the Lord added to their number daily those who were being saved.[3]

Now we're talking about how our need for relationship is satisfied in community, so before we go any deeper into these verses, we'd better define what community is. You'll be blown away when you learn what it means. *Community* means—man, I'm so excited I get to be the one to tell you this—people gathering together.

I'll give you a minute to clean your mind off the wall.

Seriously, though, God's Word doesn't really give us an earth-shattering concept of what community *is*. Rather, God wants to show us what a godly community *does*. And when a godly community *does* certain things, it's called church.

What's interesting is that when people gather together *as the church*, the definition of community expands in wild and amazing new dimensions. Every ethnicity and race and culture. Rich and poor and middle class. Suburban and urban and rural. Politically liberal and conservative and everything in between. Old and young. Highly educated and less educated. What links them together is Jesus and how they live and act because of Jesus.

Do our local churches always look like this? Definitely not—to our discredit! We're way too homogenized and pasteurized and ghettoized.

But our churches could look like this. And they should.

---

3 Acts 2:42-47.

And sometimes they do. I can't think of a better witness to the truth and love of God than a church that's genuinely a reflection of its host culture.

The reason we're spending so much time defining church community is that we're learning about how to live outward. And what our hurting world needs is for the people of God to be the people of God. To be church. Unfortunately, just as we've all been through painful, difficult things in relationships, most of us have been through that stuff at church as well. Our churches aren't perfect because they're filled with *us*. We've got to remember that the church, according to God's Word, is the bride of Christ. And getting ready for the wedding isn't all sunshine and roses. There's drama and behind-the-scenes fighting. Arguments and hurt feelings. Plus the "wedding" between the church and Christ isn't on Sunday mornings, either—it's at the end of history.

So everything we do before that? Wedding prep.

The problem with the churches we are a part of is the problem with every church, in every place, at every time. We're not there yet. History is still happening. All of us are in process. We're messy. And yet . . . God's plan is the church! Not just his plan to satisfy our need for relationship but his plan for all of humanity.

With that in mind, let's dig into our verses about the early church. It was a community that focused on four things— the apostle's doctrine, fellowship, the breaking of bread, and prayers—which are what God wants to see all of us engaging in through our communities.

God's Word

Community is rooted in God's Word. (Yes, this means the Bible, which is what our verses talk about, and also it means Jesus, who is the eternal Word.)

In the world of the early church, the Bible looked very different. What we call the Old Testament was the Jewish Scriptures. It was, to borrow a great title from Philip Yancey, *The Bible Jesus Read*.

So the early church continued to study their Bible—the Old Testament—and they soaked up the teaching and doctrine of the apostles. The names we're familiar with from the books of the New Testament, like Peter and James and John, were alive and well. They'd spent the previous three years doing everything with Jesus, and they knew him and his teaching better than anyone.

Then there was Paul, the unlikeliest missionary ever. He'd spent his career hunting down the followers of Jesus and tossing them in jail—or worse. So naturally God chose *him* to spread the church around the known world, plus author some of the most profound books in the New Testament.

That's what was going on with the phrase "devoted themselves to the apostles' teaching." They were studying God's truth whenever and wherever they could, and they were doing it together.

Circling back to our own communities, we get God's truth from God's Word and from other people who have been transformed by God's Word. That's why the Bible is the most beloved, most reviled, most useful, most attacked, most read, most contested, most controversial, most precious book in history—because God's Word *tells it like it is.*

It tells *everything* like it is. You cannot read the Bible and not be challenged. The Bible lays out for us who God is and who we are, and it tells us what's going to happen now *and* at the end of history. Those are some major claims!

If you want to base your life on another book, even a famous one like Plato's *Republic* or Kanye's collected lyrics, no one is going to bat an eye. But if you base your life on a book that claims to be *the* book, for all people in all cultures in all times?

Expect resistance.

Quick example. Pretty much everyone wants to love people. Our culture tells us to love people by letting them do whatever they want, as long as it doesn't "hurt anyone." We talked earlier in this book about how God says that sometimes loving people means challenging them. That's the kind of countercultural message that is either life-giving or closed-minded, depending on how you see the world.

This is why we pursue God's Word in community. We encourage one another and give one another strength.

Peter uses a cool image for how God's Word begins to change us. He's like, "Babies grow by doing one thing: drinking their mothers' milk. You're baby Christians, so do the same thing and drink the pure milk of God's Word."[4]

The Bible also calls itself "bread" and "meat." Taken together, those images tell us that God's Word is what we

---

[4] 1 Peter 2:2 (author's paraphrase).

need to live on no matter what stage of life we're in. It's nourishment that produces growth. Remember in chapter 1.4 when we looked at Psalm 1? We want to be "like a tree planted by streams of water, which yields its fruit in season and whose leaf does not wither" (verse 3). Why? Because whatever we do will prosper! And who is that person? The one whose "delight is in the law of the LORD, and who meditates on his law day and night" (verse 2).

This is the reason the church that Bill Ritchie founded forty years ago—Crossroads Community, where I have the pleasure to be a pastor—preaches through entire books of the Bible and usually through groups of books in order, one after another. We might prefer to avoid certain books or certain topics, but we need our milk and bread and meat!

In community we need to read God's Word and discover what it says, what we think it means—prayerfully and humbly—and how to start living.

Which produces growth and discipleship in a community, because when we understand God more, act more like Jesus, and listen to the leading of the Spirit more, we naturally pass that on to others.

Fellowship

What fellowship basically means is having things in common and taking care of one another—and in the case of the early church, it was having *all* things in common.

That's different from how a lot of our churches "fellowship"—having coffee and donuts after the service!

In our verses, though, we learn that part of how the early

church fellowshipped was to identify needs within the community and then immediately address that need, by choice.

I can legitimately brag about Crossroads in this area. It seems like every week I hear about a need that was met by the church community. Someone will ask if I heard so-and-so was in the hospital, but then right away tell me not to worry because there's already a rotation of people who are visiting regularly, another group of people who have organized a meal plan for them, and another group of people who are watching the kids.

That's how biblical community is meant to function. But "*all* the believers were together and had everything in common"[5] describes vanishingly few of our churches in the twenty-first-century West. So let's ask ourselves something: What would the world think if it saw the church actually, actively, joyfully taking care of itself?

This isn't about politics, even though it's hard for us to avoid filtering it through that lens. I'll throw out some terms that you may or may not have been thinking. *Handouts. Socialism. Welfare. Dependency.* Okay, now it's your turn to take those terms and throw them out! Because really what's at stake here is our basic willingness to help people. That's it. That invitation is all throughout the Bible, from start to finish. If we see a need, we're invited to be the agent of change. To meet that need. It's always relational and contextual. We're choosing to help a specific person with a specific need at a specific time. We can worry about tomorrow tomorrow.

---

[5] Acts 2:44 (emphasis added).

In fact, God's Word is completely realistic on the human condition here. In 2 Thessalonians, for example, Paul tells the church, "Look, there are some people in your church who are lazy. They're taking advantage of your generosity and just coasting. That's why the rule should be, 'If you won't work, you won't eat.' You can't *force* them to work, but do everything in your power to help them become productive. That way they can help others, just as you've helped them. However it goes down, though, never give up on doing good. You won't regret it" (author's paraphrase).

Being human means having needs—and when we have real needs, the church is meant to spring into action to meet those needs.

It's fascinating that we've made *needy* a synonym for *poor*. But *all* of us are needy, even the wealthiest! When the richest person in your church loses a child, what good is their money? And don't forget that Jesus regards the "poor in spirit" as blessed!

I want to be clear that God's Word doesn't destroy or condemn the idea of personal belongings or money. It assumes we will have those things, at least to an extent. What it does invite each of us to do, however, is ask a life-changing question: *What will I do with my belongings and money?*

See the difference? The believers in the early church *chose* to provide for one another. They wanted to sell property, for example, and give the money to someone in need. They didn't have to . . . they *got* to! Galatians 6:10 says, "Therefore, as we have opportunity, let us do good to all people, especially to those who belong to the family of believers." Imagine if we lived out that invitation!

Note too that the priority seems to be those "inside" the church. But of course that doesn't mean the church community isn't meant to move outward, into a hurting world. The life of Jesus, not to mention most of the New Testament, contradicts that isolationism. What this does mean, though, is that a healthy church community is best able to bring health to a sick world. It reminds me of when the airlines tell parents to put on their own oxygen masks before helping their children.

When the church is acting like the church, it creates a unique community that joyfully and creatively takes care of its own needs, as well as the needs of other groups. The church is a network. A matrix of organic relationships. When a need is known, that need is met.

That's exactly why we need to be plugged in! Because it's possible, in any church, to remain on the periphery. Relationships can't be legislated. If we don't engage and share, the community won't know how to help us and we won't know whom *we* can help. Diving in to the life of a true community is frightening. We will be part of relationships we can't control—relationships that go beyond common interests and all the way to the core of who we are as people.

But if we choose to dive in, we'll be smack in the middle of what God is doing.

Fellowship is messy. It's a process. It's personal. And it's exactly what church—what true community—is meant to be.

Breaking of Bread

This part is so simple and so good.

"They broke bread in their homes and ate together with glad and sincere hearts."

We can all get behind eating meals together!

This could be talking about sharing Communion. It could be talking about a good old-fashioned church potluck.[6] Probably it's both. And probably more overlapping than we're used to. Our Communion meal is really "food" in name only, right? We're not going to invite someone over and give them a tiny bit of matzo and a baby-sized sip of grape juice. But if there were steaming hot, crusty, fresh-baked loaves of bread on the table? And a nice bottle of wine? We're going to want to break bread together as often as possible.

Look what comes right before this verse: "Every day they continued to meet together in the temple courts." So they gathered together, fellowshipping and soaking themselves in God's Word, and then they kept the party going! *Want to come to my house today? Let's go to Peter's house tomorrow . . . he's got the crustiest bread!*

They were "devoted" to these things for a reason: These things were awesome! The community was giving them life and love and godly friendships. Purpose. Their hearts were being warmed by genuine relationships. Why *wouldn't* they be devoted to that?

But you're busy. You're overscheduled. Maxed out and mixed up. You don't have time to devote yourself to anything new.

---

[6] Reminds me of a joke. How many Christians does it take to change a light bulb? Ten. One to change the bulb and nine to plan the potluck.

Except the only person in charge of your schedule is you. Seriously. There are outside responsibilities, sure. If you have a job, you're probably not in control of about one-third of your time. (Although even at work you may be able to choose what you do during lunch, what you have on your desk, what you talk about at break time, and so on.) Sleep accounts for another third of our time. But that still leaves you with eight hours a day. You can choose to fill those eight hours with Netflix or the Yankees or walks with your dog. And those might be good choices.

But every yes is a no to something else. We've got to ask, "God, am I prioritizing the things you prioritize?"

What I'm *not* saying is that all your free time should be spent at church. Remember, the believers in our verses came together at church and then went out into the community, to homes and businesses and markets.

Let's make the time to break bread. If we're ruthless with cutting things *out* of our schedules—neutral or even good things—we can have more space for godly community.

I love how Hebrews 10:24-25 puts it: "And let us consider how we may spur one another on toward love and good deeds, not giving up meeting together, as some are in the habit of doing, but encouraging one another."

When we prioritize biblical community, we're not only happier, but we also become better, more Christlike versions of ourselves. We *need* community. We need the relationships, yes—but even more we need to be spurred on by others. We don't get more like Jesus on our own. We don't get holier staying safe in our houses and apartments, listening to the Christian radio station 24-7.

Plus, that's not what the world needs from us either. There's too much pain out there for us to stick our heads in the sand and wait for Jesus to come back.

Prayers

Community is where we start to pray praises.

I know that's a tongue twister, but it's a good way to remember what our conversations with God and one another should sound like.

Too often we get fixated on our requests. Talking to God becomes nothing more than a way of listing our problems. "God, thank you for this day. Please help me get more money for groceries, and I need some new gutters because I hung too many Christmas lights on them and they sagged off the roof, and help me to get Johnny to do his homework right when he gets home from school, and please help . . . "

The list goes on and on. But here's the thing: Every day of our lives we *could* pray a gigantic list of needs and wants and requests. We'll never *not* have that junk in our lives.

But is that how Jesus taught his disciples to pray? Is it how the early church prayed? Is it how the great prayers of the Bible sound?[7]

Community reminds us of the blessings we already enjoy. It reminds and encourages us to pray *praises* and not just requests.

How does a prayer like this sound? We all have our own

---

[7] If you want your mind and heart blown open when it comes to prayer, then try reading some of the greatest hits in God's Word. Check out 1 Samuel 1, Psalm 51, Habakkuk 3, Psalm 139, Luke 1:46-55, and . . . okay, I'd better stop.

ways of praying, but I'd say something like this: *God, this hurts. I don't know what's going to happen. But, God, thank you for being with me. I know you'll never leave nor forsake me. I know you've got me in this.*

Look what it says at the end of verse 47: "praising God and enjoying the favor of all the people."

Everything the early church has been doing—studying the Word, fellowshipping, sharing meals together—leads to prayer and a spirit of joyful thankfulness. They can't help but praise God. Praise is the fruit, even in the midst of difficulty.

I love how praise becomes the best way to witness to unbelievers. We read that God "added to their number daily those who were being saved." These Christians were going into town to meet at the temple, which had more relationship to something like a bandstand in the park or a community plaza, by the way, than to our modern church campuses. Then they were going to one another's homes. And their lives were so filled with joy and warmth and love that they couldn't keep their mouths shut!

So what other people in the city heard weren't angry sermons on the street corners or lists of stuff that was wrong. Instead they heard the community *praising*.

God has been so good to me this week! First there was that situation where . . .

. . . and that's *why I'm still so grateful, because . . .*

I can't even explain exactly why, but I feel at peace with the news from the doctor. I know God's will is best.

People are hearing this stuff and, unsurprisingly, are attracted to it! We need relationships. We're meant to be in community. And any community that is functioning as a true community will attract new people.

Only a healthy church can praise in the midst of trouble—and that's the kind of prayer that can change someone's life. Community shares strength, the kind of strength that comes from God in the midst of our human weakness.

Memorize this scripture. I guarantee you won't regret it—plus it's like three verses for the price of one! "Rejoice always, pray continually, give thanks in all circumstances; for this is God's will for you in Christ Jesus" (1 Thessalonians 5:16-18).

This is another great summary of what biblical community does. Who wouldn't want to be part of something like this? We *can't* rejoice always and give thanks in all circumstances *unless* we're in a Jesus-centered community. It would be nonsensical.

Your community of fellow sports fans? Or your community of political junkies or business leaders or parents? You can't rejoice without ceasing unless the center of your community is Jesus. He's the only one who understands our mess, meets us in that mess, and works within and without us to redeem that mess.

Praise God.

Redefining Church

Before we close this section, I want to say something I *know* many of you are thinking. Maybe this is you.

> *That's great, Fusco. Good for you. I mean it—you've got a good thing going at your church. Keep it up. But me? Going to some mega-worship-center-with-a-coffee-bar*

isn't for me. I've been burned by the institutional
church. That's not something I can do. I love Jesus, but I
just meet with some friends every week to read the Word
and pray. We share meals with one another and then
help feed the homeless. We're not going to get stuck, you
know? We respond to Jesus, not some hierarchy that's just
as likely to hurt people as help them.

If that's you, here's the thing: *You're still being the church.*
Yes you, the one who swore to never "join the church" again.
So keep it up!

No matter what shape our church communities take, from five people to five thousand, those communities are God's design for us. But let's encourage one another to love the people of God who embrace a different community style than we prefer. We are all still family in Jesus!

As we live outward, let's remember that our hurting world needs the church to *be* the church. We love the world by being the church. My prayer is that in the power of God's Spirit we become the most beautiful, grace-filled, creative version of the church we can be.

We need everyone's help. Everyone needs our help. So let's do it together, in the name of Jesus.

Practice

Find a church and become an integral part of it. There are no other practical steps.

Seriously. This is everything. God's family is where our need for relationship is satisfied and where the world's need for Jesus is met. There's no such thing as Christianity without church. It's like claiming to be a professional soccer player without a team.

Church can be a hard pill to swallow in our individualistic age, especially the more we learn about the failings of various churches or church leaders. Those aren't failures of *church*, though. They're failures of *people*, and they happen outside the church too.

So find a church and get involved. Don't live on the periphery. Join the family and roll up your sleeves.

3.4

↑ ↙ ↗

compassion / generosity

Problem

This book has been like a road trip through parts of God's Word, hasn't it? And now we've reached the final part of our journey into the Jesus way of living.

This art of living is simply doing life God's way. We're living upward, loving God with all our hearts. We're living inward, seeing and loving ourselves in light of who Jesus is and what he's done for us. And we're living outward into the world, through God's Spirit, loving our neighbors. Our lives are characterized by justice and creativity and community.

Following Jesus with our lives doesn't just mean we think differently than our culture does. Jesus doesn't give us a new *understanding* of life. Not exactly. Jesus gives us a new way of actually *living* in the world. God living in and through us produces a radical new way of working, speaking, loving, and—as we'll see in this final chapter—giving.

People notice. And it makes an amazing difference in the world.

Let's start with a quick story.

There was a kid in our town, Teagan, all of nine years old, who wanted to collect twenty-five thousand pairs of shoes for a nonprofit. She'd seen a television show about kids not being able to go to school because they didn't have the prerequisite shoes. She decided that that needed to change, and she wanted to give the shoes she collected to kids in America and around the world who couldn't afford them. She'd gathered *tons* of pairs from family members, friends, and businesses, all of which she stored in her garage. But the going was slow, and she was starting to get discouraged . . . plus, the garage was running out of space!

I heard about Teagan's story at a local business that had agreed to become one of her drop-off spots for the shoes. Our church decided it would be cool to help out this little world changer. We asked if we could tell our congregation about her idea and see if they wanted to pitch in.

Eighteen thousand pairs of donated shoes later, we had a pile in the church lobby that was six feet tall for weeks, even as we were removing thousands of pairs of shoes each week and storing them in a trailer. We have some great pictures of Teagan sitting on top of this enormous pile of shoes—and by the way, she exceeded her goal!

I love what Teagan's mom said: "She definitely has a big heart and cares a lot about kids who are less fortunate. Things like this are going to be a part of her life for a long, long time."[1]

Our world greatly needs compassionate people like Teagan. People who see others and spring into action. Because God's way of blessing the world is through our generosity.

When we realize that everything we have is meant to be a blessing to *us* as we use it to bless *others*, we step into God's perfect plans for our lives. And as we'll see in this chapter, Teagan's mom is right. If compassion leads us to generous action, we're setting our lives on a certain course.

Our world needs compassion, and we need to *be* people of compassion. Deep down, we all have this core desire to be a part of something bigger. We have this drive to be in a community that is self-giving and nurturing. It's like how businesses today often emphasize a transformative component in their product. It's one thing to buy shoes, but it's something else entirely to buy a pair of shoes that *also* gives a pair of shoes to someone in need. No matter what you believe, being a force for good brings joy!

God created us with this longing to be compassionate— to be people who can be moved by the Spirit to see the needs of others and then act on their behalf. We're built to follow the golden rule: *If I was in trouble, I'd want someone to help me. So I'm going to help that person who's in trouble.* All around us we see chances to alleviate suffering. To change lives and restore families and make life more beautiful.

---

[1] Adam Littman, "Youngster with Sole Collects Thousands of Pairs of Shoes," *The Columbian*, April 1, 2015, www.columbian.com/news/2015/mar/31/youngster-with-sole-collects-thousands-of-pairs-of.

And God's Word teaches us the way to meet our need for compassion and for compassionate action: generosity.

Now here's something obviously true, at least once we say it out loud: We can give to others only what we have received. Whether we're talking about physical gifts we can give, like money,[2] or spiritual gifts we can give, like kindness or patience, we've got to *have* it to *give* it.

Which is why this is our last chapter. We know that it's only by living upward, inward, and *then* outward can we produce the kind of lasting fruit that comes from God. Life inspired and led by the Holy Spirit means a life of radical generosity.

And really it's the life we all want, even if it sounds scary. Our world needs more Teagans. Our world needs *us*.

Promise

Before we read our scripture for this chapter, let me set the scene.

Our story happens pretty soon after Jesus returns to heaven. Pentecost, when God's Spirit goes crazy in Jerusalem, has happened, and there are new, vibrant Christian communities springing up all across the Mediterranean. The church in Jerusalem, though, is having a tough time. That's still the center of power for the folks who arrested and killed Jesus. It's a city of entrenched tradition, unlike some of the more cosmopolitan communities outside Palestine.

---

[2] Yes, I'm going to talk about money in this chapter. Generosity will include our finances, of course, but it won't be limited to them. We'll continually find new ways of giving generously. Heck, by the time we're done with this chapter, we might wish we were *only* talking about money!

Since the Jerusalem Christians are being severely perse-cuted, Paul gets the idea to take a collection for them. So Paul goes around to his missionary partners and other churches scattered around the Mediterranean, and he says, "Hey, we've got to collect some money for the Christians in Jerusalem. They're getting hammered, and a lot of us are much more comfortable than they are. So let's get this thing done and help them out."

That takes us to our passage, where Paul is writing to the church in the city of Corinth and thanking them for being willing to pitch in. But it's not all sunshine with Corinth, because although they've committed to help the believers in Jerusalem, they haven't actually done it yet. They said they were eager to help, but so far they haven't collected anything.

Okay, let's read our scripture. It comes from Paul's second letter to the church in Corinth:

> There is no need for me to write to you about
> this service to the Lord's people. For I know your
> eagerness to help, and I have been boasting about
> it to the Macedonians, telling them that since last
> year you in Achaia were ready to give; and your
> enthusiasm has stirred most of them to action. But
> I am sending the brothers in order that our boasting
> about you in this matter should not prove hollow,
> but that you may be ready, as I said you would be.
> For if any Macedonians come with me and find you
> unprepared, we—not to say anything about you—
> would be ashamed of having been so confident. So

I thought it necessary to urge the brothers to visit you in advance and finish the arrangements for the generous gift you had promised. Then it will be ready as a generous gift, not as one grudgingly given.

Remember this: Whoever sows sparingly will also reap sparingly, and whoever sows generously will also reap generously. Each of you should give what you have decided in your heart to give, not reluctantly or under compulsion, for God loves a cheerful giver. And God is able to bless you abundantly, so that in all things at all times, having all that you need, you will abound in every good work.[3]

Don't you love how human the stories in God's Word are? I sure do.

Here we see a real person dealing with a real issue but showing us how to do it in a godly way that produces growth. Paul is telling the believers in Corinth that they are off to an amazing start . . . but he has a few ideas about how they can get over the finish line. And he goes further, encouraging them that their giving will be an even bigger blessing than they expected.

It reminds me a lot of our culture. We want to be compassionate people, but most of us can use some help getting our rears in gear. Having a willingness and a passion to help is great. If we've already got that, praise God!

But now we've got to walk our talk.

---

[3] 2 Corinthians 9:1-8.

Compassion is meant to move us to action, so if all we have are good intentions—like enough to pave the road to you-know-where—that's insufficient. James 2:15-16 asks rhetorically, "Suppose a brother or a sister is without clothes and daily food. If one of you says to them, 'Go in peace; keep warm and well fed,' but does nothing about their physical needs, what good is it?"

The church in Corinth was actually so passionate, so willing to help, that they started to get other churches on board. The word got around on whatever the first-century equivalent of Facebook was, and pretty soon there was a line out the door to help out the church in Jerusalem.[4]

That's why Paul tells the Corinthians that he's sending some folks to "finish the arrangements for the generous gift" the church had promised. Partly because he didn't want the church to be embarrassed. He knew there was a good chance that all those good intentions wouldn't do a single bit of good for the church in Jerusalem. Also, Paul himself didn't want to be embarrassed! He'd been bragging about how zealous and generous the Corinthians were. He didn't want to be hanging out with the other apostles somewhere and have them be like, "Hey, Paul, about that 'generous' church of yours . . ."

As we continue the chapter, we're going to unpack all of this in more detail, but I'm going to try something a little different. We're going to start with some practical ideas about how to be generous. Why? Because when it comes to

[4] By the way, next time you're driving to work, ask yourself this fun question: Who is the twenty-first-century equivalent of the persecuted church in Jerusalem?

generosity, we can apply the classic business advice "If you fail to plan, you plan to fail."

Our selfish culture makes for a great deal of "generosity inertia." So before we study any more about generosity, I want to try to convince you that it's possible to actually *be* generous people.

With that in mind, here are three practical, doable steps we can take toward generosity.

1. Simplify

If we want to be generous and compassionate, we've got to start by simplifying.

And guess what? We *want* to simplify! We all do. I haven't met one person in my community who's like, "Fusco, can you help me complicate my life? I just don't have enough stuff or enough going on."

We love our toys, whether we're kids or adults. We love our vacations and hobbies and leagues. We love our full bookshelves and technology and overflowing garages.

But everything we acquire takes at least some of our time and money. And everything we do takes at least some of our time.

Simplifying helps us free up time and money that we can use to be generous. Put another way, if we aren't regularly asking questions about how we can simplify our lives, we probably aren't being as generous as we could be.

Leave it to God to make one thing we want (simplifying our lives) a step toward another thing we want (being generous)!

2. Start small . . . but actually start

I meet people all the time who ask me, "How did I get here?"

They're struggling with some issue, or they feel adrift. They want to be different—more plugged in to God's family, more generous—but they feel stuck. The crazy thing is, I almost always know the answer to how they got there, even if I don't know them.

"You got here," I say, "because you're not being proactive. You're reacting to everything that gets thrown your way instead of getting out in front of it."

Take anything you want to change. Want to lose seventy pounds? Start by losing one pound! It's the same with generosity. People tell me they want to start being more generous with their time or money. "But, Pastor, how do I start? Tell me what to do."

I always tell them to pick something, start small, and then actually *do* it. Say they want to give some of their money to help build God's Kingdom. I tell them it doesn't matter if it's a dollar a month or a million bucks a year. That's not rhetorical, by the way—I mean it quite literally.

See, everything we have is a gift of God. That's the big point: It's all *God's*. And God wants everything from us. Not 10 percent of our money. Not our Sunday mornings. God wants it *all*!

That's why we can start anywhere, even with something seemingly insignificant. What matters is that we're willing and that we start moving forward in faith. We're planning to become more like Jesus, so we start taking steps, even small ones, in that direction.

When we do that, we discover that God is faithful too. Remember, God doesn't promise to lay out everything in our lives so we can see it and give our stamp of approval. God promises to take care of our needs every day and give us new mercy and new grace for tomorrow.

When I got out of college, I wanted to start giving money to God. I was making a few bucks here and there playing gigs, but I didn't have a steady job. I'd be sitting in church, watching the offering plate come toward me, and glancing down at my wallet. There would be a wrinkly five-dollar bill in there, and I'd think, *I could put that in the plate, but it's also like five rolls of toilet paper.* And I had to pay rent and car insurance, and buy food.[5] But by faith, I would toss my cash in the plate.

But you know what? Looking back, I always had toilet paper. (Or I had something that worked in place of toilet paper. But I digress.)

Start small. But be faithful. Take that little flame and tend it. See how God wants to grow it. Then continually take the next small step forward . . . until you're ready to take the leap!

3. Prioritize

This is a scary one. I'm going to suggest we give to God and God's Kingdom *first*, before we give to ourselves. And I'm going to suggest we follow that principle with our time and our money.

We humans have always struggled with this. Way back

---

5 When you are in your twenties, instant ramen counts as actual food.

when the ancient Israelites were learning how to be generous, God taught them a principle called "first fruits." Say they had just brought in the harvest for the year. Before they stored it or milled the grain or saved some to plant the following year, they were to give some of it to God.

At the end of the day, God asks us to step forward in faith. To give *before* we keep. And it's after we step into the unknown that God meets us and provides for us. If we give only out of our excess, and give only once we've taken care of ourselves, we're not really giving.

So if you want to give money, for example, *give it right after you get your paycheck.* And if you want to give time, for example, schedule it in first. When you plan your monthly calendar on that whiteboard in the kitchen, write down the ways you're going to be generous first. Write down the things you're committing to for God. *Then* add in the PTA meeting. Take a look and see if your mah-jongg club still fits. (Before the mah-jongg lobby tries to get this book banned, I'm not saying mah-jongg is wrong to play.[6] What I am saying is that we're never going to look back at the end of our lives and wish we'd spent more time matching little ivory tiles with cool colored patterns on them.)

Something has to take priority in our schedules and our wallets. God is asking us to trust him that putting *his* things first is the best thing for us and for our world.

Remember, Paul tells the Corinthians to act the way they've been speaking.

---

[6] Actually, if there *is* a mah-jongg lobby that could get this book banned, go for it! Banned books sell like hotcakes.

We're like that too sometimes. Maybe we had a certain commitment that we gave up on, or we told someone we wanted to be involved without doing anything about it. The temptation is to make sure we don't see that person, right? Out of sight, out of mind.

An unwillingness to make a commitment *and* follow through on it is a sign of immaturity. But it's understandable in our culture. We're all about being noncommittal. To make ourselves feel better, though, we talk about being noncommittal in positive terms. We're being "open" or "chill." We're not "stuck in a rut." We're "ready for whatever happens."

Trouble is, nine times out of ten the next thing that randomly happens to us isn't the best, most godly, most Kingdom-building thing.

If we truly want to be people who bless the world as Jesus did, we need to simplify, start small, and prioritize.

Generous Legacy

And here's the thing when it comes to generosity: We've got to start right now. Not just because the world needs us now, but because of our legacies.

Me, I'm at that in-between age in life, where thinking about a concept like "legacy" isn't exactly crazy, but it's not totally natural, either. Part of me still feels like a college kid, and another part of me has achy knees coming down the stairs every morning. If you're firmly on the achy-knee side of things, you'll be right with me here on the legacy stuff. If you sprint down stairs and think you're immortal, pay attention.

We need to consider our legacy.

How will we be remembered when we're gone? Do we want to be truly awesome or forgettable and lame? Do we want Jesus to call us good and faithful, or do we want people to shrug and be like, "They died? Meh . . . "

If we know what end goal we want, we can design our lives around that goal. Because being awesome isn't going to happen by accident.

This doesn't mean that we need to become superstars starting tomorrow, so that we'll be super-duper stars by the time we die. Rather, considering our legacy means taking the steps we can, each day, to become more like Jesus.

Remember in the last chapter, how the early church devoted themselves to soaking in God's Word, fellowshipping, sharing meals together, praying, and praising—and how, because of all that, they did tons of great things in their communities? That's legacy building. Or the story we started this chapter with, where Teagan did something generous and compassionate? Same deal: She's building her legacy. We're talking about the kind of small, everyday actions produced by simplifying and prioritizing.

I want to connect this idea of considering our legacy with something surprising and—I hope—practically helpful.

Have you ever heard someone claim they know when Jesus is coming back? Then, after it doesn't happen, the pastor or leader backpedals and says maybe they got the calculations wrong . . . but *next* time they'll nail it! Truth is, if someone claims to know when Jesus is coming back, they're flat wrong. It's impossible to know.

More importantly, it's irrelevant! Why? Because we should

be living every day of our lives in light of Jesus' return. The day Jesus returns is the day our legacies freeze.

This is definitely not a lame carpe diem thing, I promise. We usually say "carpe diem" when we want to spoil ourselves or get away with something. It's not usually "Should we go serve soup at the homeless shelter? Carpe diem!"

What I'm talking about is living each day like it's our last *by simply responding to and following Jesus.*

The early church became embodiments of Jesus in the world. If you'd told them, some random Tuesday, that it was their last day on earth, I don't think they would have regretted gathering, fellowshipping, and praising—just as they wouldn't have regretted speaking kindly to a neighbor on the way home or sharing some food with the beggar outside the marketplace.

Our legacies start today.

And the things that will determine our legacies are small, faithful steps of generosity toward others, in the name of Jesus.

Right now, today, the return of Jesus is closer now than it has *ever* been. Sure, it's only *one* day closer than yesterday, but still!

Now is the time. This is the moment. We need to be prepared. We need to be awake and alert, not slumbering in our tiny selfish distractions and concerns. God's Spirit wakes us up. That's what he does in our lives. We've been given the most important job imaginable, and some of us have our feet up on the desk. We're snoozing.

Recently my wife and I have been having conversations

about making sure our family isn't asleep when it comes to Kingdom generosity. Life defaults to being overscheduled, right? If we're not being proactive about living outward, generously, we're going to fail.

So we've been asking ourselves questions: "What can we do this year as a family?" "What does generosity look like for the Fuscos during this season of life?" "What's the next step?" "Is there anything we need to simplify or cancel?" "What are we teaching our kids? And what are they teaching us?" "Are there things we feel passionate about that we aren't activating?"

We've got to re-up on this stuff. We've got to stay awake.

Sow Generously

This section is going to be short and sweet. It's actually something of a counterpoint to what I said before about taking small steps.

After Paul goes over the details of the donation for the church in Jerusalem, he gives the Corinthians a bit of earthy wisdom. Back then, everyone would have nodded along with this, even if they lived in a city. They were "farm to table" before it was cool, right?

> Remember this: Whoever sows sparingly will also reap sparingly, and whoever sows generously will also reap generously. Each of you should give what you have decided in your heart to give, not reluctantly or under compulsion, for God loves a cheerful giver. And God is able to bless you abundantly, so that in

all things at all times, having all that you need, you
will abound in every good work.[7]

I'm going to level with you: There wasn't much agricul-
tural sowing happening in my suburban Jersey neighborhood. I know New Jersey is called the Garden State, but not
where I grew up!

But what this scripture is saying is that all else being equal,
the more seed you put into the ground, the better harvest
you're going to get. It makes sense. And I love how this same
picture of sowing and reaping is used for other things in the
Bible. Like if you "sow" seeds of rebellion against God, you're
going to reap more sin as the harvest.

So if we want to reap a significant harvest from our
generosity, we need to sow significantly. We need to make
significant investments! Whether we're investing our time,
talent, or treasure—which is a great shortcut for thinking of
categories of generosity—are we doing it sparingly? Or are
we being generous and bountiful, even beyond our comfort
level, because we trust that God is far more generous than
we can ever be?

You will never meet a follower of Jesus who says at the end
of their days, "I gave too much. I served too much. I prayed
too much. I was too generous. Why, oh *why*, didn't I spend
more time tweaking the lineup of my fantasy football team?"

In Galatians 5, Paul lists what he calls the fruit of the
Spirit—actions that are produced by God's Spirit working

---

[7] 2 Corinthians 9:6-8.

in and through us. You might be familiar with the list: "love, joy, peace, patience, kindness, goodness, faithfulness, gentleness and self-control." Paul says something intriguing right after that list: "Against such things there is no law."[8] That sounds more like something Yoda would say, but what it means is that doing these things is never wrong. We can't do them enough. We will never regret being kind or loving or self-controlled.

Here's how this harmonizes with taking small steps. We take small steps as we're learning something new—but as we increase our skill or become more comfortable, we do more. What Paul is saying is that we can't afford to sow *sparingly*. Just as we can't afford to sow reluctantly or because we think we have to. We're meant to grow in our giving.

With generosity as with life, we get out what we put in. We all know that.

And if you want Jesus spirituality, be generous. Be Jesus to someone. Prioritize the Kingdom and see who shows up.

Church Is God's Chosen Vehicle

To this point we've been talking about individuals.

But don't forget, our whole conversation started with the church in Corinth helping the church in Jerusalem. At the end of the day, generosity is a church-level concept. Which is uncomfortable. Because a lot of us who want to follow Jesus and make a difference are also skeptical of the church.

The church does have problems, yes. One of the biggest

---

[8] Galatians 5:22-23.

is that there are new churches starting up all the time in this country, and most of their members come from *existing* churches! What the church is *meant* to be is a vehicle for God's grace in the world, for the sake of the world and the glory of God. It's tragic when we can communicate only with other believers.

The church is salt. The church is light. The church is a fruitful vineyard. The church is a radiant bride. But we make our churches into bunkers.

Part of this is the contemporary willingness to criticize the church and religion. We get much more bad press now, which is a good thing! Let's put our cards on the table: child abuse, financial scandals, immoral leaders. Too often those things have been covered up or explained away. That's wrong.

And it's why you hear, "I'm spiritual, and Jesus was a good teacher, but he didn't come to start an institutional church." "Organized religion is bad for the world." "Think of all the evil done in the name of religion!"

I've got to be blunt here. Like, this is my last chapter, so I'm just going to say it: Rejecting the church because of particular sins it has committed doesn't add up. It's not just apples and oranges . . . it's more like apples and tennis balls. Of *course* organized religion has done some bad things! The church is made up of people. But when the Christian church participates in some evil, it's doing so *against* its own teachings and goals and against the explicit example and message of Jesus.

But think about the evil done in the name of secular causes. Communism, fascism. Capitalism. Heck, even democracy. Communism alone caused 94 *million* civilian deaths in the twentieth century.[9] On purpose.

It's been said that the Christian church is the only global institution devoted to the welfare of its *non*members. That's incredible! The people of God, the global church, are responsible for an almost infinite amount of good and godly works. Hospitals, orphanages, relief organizations, clean water, science, fighting slavery and trafficking, economic development, fine art . . . I could go on and on here. The church, taken as a whole, has consistently helped the world's most vulnerable and weak. That is the real legacy of the church, and don't let anyone claim otherwise.

Now here's our last word on compassionate generosity: "And God is able to bless you abundantly, so that in all things at all times, having all that you need, you will abound in every good work."

That's the end of our passage. That's the end of our movement on living outward. And that, friends, is the art of living.

Read that verse five or six times right now, nice and slow. I'll wait.

starts tapping foot and playing air guitar

Okay, that's amazing, right?

We are an extension of *God* in the world. We are the church, the family of God. The generous community of God. Yes, we fail. Yes, we sin. But that does not define us. We are defined by the abundant, amazing, surprising blessing of God. God has blessed us so that we can bless others. Upward,

---

9 "20th Century Death: Selected Major Causes," Information Is Beautiful, accessed April 17, 2017, http://www.informationisbeautiful.net/visualizations/20th-century-death/.

inward, and now outward. God's Word tells us that all the nations of earth will be blessed because the church declares that God is the King of kings and walks in the way of Jesus. It's not just proclamation but also *demonstration*.

The upside-down reality of Jesus spirituality is that the more we give in God's name, the more we're filled by God's grace. We can't out-give God. We can always choose to give generously. And when God continually refills and replenishes us with his grace, we don't need to hoard or cling to anything.

The absolute last thing we want is to live lives devoid of impact, of purpose, of difference making.

There is zero point, Jesus reminds us, if we get everything we want in this life, only to lose our souls. And the way to save our souls—to find ourselves—is to act as the hands and feet and mouth of Jesus in the world. All through God's provision.

That's a legacy of generous grace and goodness we will never regret.

Will you follow Jesus and learn the art of living? Will you love God with all your heart, soul, strength, and mind, and love your neighbor as yourself?

We're going to be learning these things our whole lives, until we draw our last breath . . .

postlude

. . . and then we'll draw a new breath.

The first breath of the rest of our forever lives.

It will be a breath of wonder. And awe. And flat-out, full-bodied joy. We'll be face-to-face with the author and perfecter of our faith. The creator and sustainer of Jesus spirituality. The one who showed us the art of living so that we could live with him.

And we'll hear, "Well done, good and faithful servant."

Those will be words of absolute affirmation—that we were true light in a dark world.

Words of complete comfort—that practicing the art of living wasn't a waste of time but was the best possible way to live.

Words of finished redemption—that our lives were thin places, where God's love could touch us and touch others through us.

Words of love—that whatever we did out of compassion for others, we did for Jesus, because he first loved us.

Words of boundless, abundant joy.

He came that we might have life and have it to the full. Life now, and life forever.

Every day of our lives he is inviting us: "Come closer. Don't be far away. Let me work in your life. You're almost home."

acknowledgments

I am thankful to God for so many people. There is truly not enough space to thank everyone who deserves it.

I want to thank my family. Lynn, Obadiah, Maranatha, and Annabelle: You all have my whole heart. To all the Fuscos, Cappadonas, Dachauers, and all the offshoots: You are the best! I am *so* blessed.

I want to thank everyone at Crossroads Community Church. I am blessed by each one of you, and I am grateful we get to simply respond to Jesus together. You are all in my heart. Special shout-outs to our founding pastor, Bill Ritchie, our servant leadership team, executive team, pastors, and staff. A huge thank-you to Margaret for helping me in every way.

I want to thank my publishing team. D. R. Jacobsen, writing with you is always a blast. Jenni Burke, you are an amazing agent and person. Don Pape, Caitlyn Carlson, Helen Macdonald, and everyone at NavPress, I love partnering with you to touch people's lives. Robin Bermel and everyone at Tyndale, thank you for all you do to help get this message out.

I want to thank my Pastor John Henry and all the Corcoran family for being such an influence on me.

Finally, if you are reading this, thank you! Thanks for being you and moving through this world with grace. And thanks for taking the time to read this. I pray that it helps in some way.

about the authors

Daniel Fusco came to a saving knowledge of Jesus Christ in April 1998 while in his last year at university. He spent a few years as a professional musician (upright and electric bass) but then felt called into pastoral ministry. He was taken on staff at Calvary Chapel Marin under the direction of Pastor John Henry Corcoran in January of 2000. In the years following his ordination in 2002, Daniel planted several churches around the country, including in New Jersey and California. In 2012, Daniel moved to Vancouver, Washington, to become the lead pastor at Crossroads Community Church, where he presently serves. He is also the founder of the Calvary Church Planting Network that helps facilitate church planters.

Daniel has taught at churches, retreats, youth rallies, leadership seminars, seminaries, college campuses, and pastors' conferences both in the States and abroad. His passion for the lost keeps him playing music and drinking coffee in and around the great city of Portland.

Daniel is blessed to be married to Lynn, and they have three children and a crazy dog. They live in southwest Washington State.

To learn more about Daniel, go to danielfusco.com.

•   •   •

D. R. Jacobsen believes "that the story of any one of us is in some measure the story of us all," a conviction that shapes his collaborative writing and editing—and a phrase of Frederick Buechner's that he's fond of stealing. He holds a BA in English from Westmont College, an MA in theology from Regent College, and an MFA in creative writing from Seattle Pacific University.

As "David Jacobsen," his essays have appeared in various journals and anthologies, and he is the author of *Rookie Dad: Thoughts on First-Time Fatherhood.* As a collaborative writer, he is represented by Don Jacobson of D. C. Jacobson & Associates. David and his wife have lived in California, Austria, and British Columbia, and now they make their home with their two boys in central Oregon. When not thinking about words, he plays pickup soccer, roots for the Timbers, and writes compelling bios. You can connect with him at jacobsenwriting.com.